You Gonna' Sell Real Estate

or *What?*

The guerrilla guide to real estate today.

By Don Phelan ©2012

Table of Contents ....…………...…. 3

Preface ……………………............................ 5

Part I – Choose your Path.
Ch. 1 – Are you thriving or surviving? 7
Ch. 2 – Swim, sink, or get out of the
water. ……………………….....……… 11
Ch. 3 – Which way do you go? ………...… 15
Ch. 4 – Measure twice, cut once ………..... 17
Ch. 5 – Make seven promises …………..... 27
Ch. 6 – Where will you fish? …………....... 33

Part II – Prospect Relentlessly.
Ch. 7 – Spread the word 37
Ch. 8 – Commit to social media ………... 53
Ch. 9 – Beat the bushes 65
Ch. 10 – Soft-sell FSBOs ……………….... 73
Ch. 11 – Target expired listings ………..... 77

Part III – Improve Your Game.
Ch. 12 – Sharpen your axe ……………..... 81
Ch. 13 – Working expireds is not
an art form …………………….. .. 93
Ch. 14 – Now is your time ……………….. 99
Ch. 15 – Prep the listing appointment ... 117
Ch. 16 – Get your listings sold. Fast … 139
Ch. 17 – Lead the pack ……………….... 143

Appendix A – Property Marketability
Checklist ………………....……... 147
About the Author ………………....…... 156
Acknowledgements …………………... 157

Preface

Make no mistake. The changes in the real estate industry over the past two decades are nothing short of revolutionary. Few industries have experienced the tsunami of change which real estate has – from the death spiral of home prices and Realtors'® earnings to the advent of instantaneous communication and social media marketing.

As with any revolution, there will be those who thrive, those who merely survive, and those who perish. If you simply hope to survive, it may be possible to do so by doing what you've always done. Possible, but not likely.

To survive – or thrive – in today's dynamic marketplace, you must change not only what you *do* but how you *think*.

> We cannot solve our
> problems with the same
> thinking we used
> when we created them.
>
> ~Albert Einstein

If you are not getting the results you want from your career, it is time to do something different. It is time to think differently. The ideas in this book will not make you a marketing expert but they will help you *think* like one – a guerrilla marketing expert. Like guerrilla warfare, guerrilla marketing employs creative tactics to win in a highly competitive environment and unforgiving landscape.

> Guerrilla marketing maintains
> that if you want to invest money,
> you can – but you don't have to if
> you are willing to invest time, energy,
> imagination and information.
>
> ~ Jay Conrad Levinson

Agents who can adapt to cultural changes of the past two decades have the opportunity to redefine and re-energize their careers. Those new to the business can build a strategy founded in the certainty of change in the future.

Part I
Choose Your Path

■■■■■■■■■■■■■■■■■■■■■■■■■■■■■■■■■■

Chapter 1
Are you thriving or surviving?

This book is about making money in a real estate career *today*, using the marketing tools and opportunities available to capture more customers and generate more income in less time.

In 2006, an agent who earned $120,000 selling roughly $4,000,000 in real estate earned net income before taxes of about $90,000. Since then:

- Housing prices have dropped 40 - 50% in many markets.

- Real estate agents hungry for income have slashed commission rates to attract clients, compelling their competitors to follow suit.

- Costs of doing business have risen dramatically.

Therefore, the cost of doing business is now a significantly greater percentage of gross revenue.

Factor in lower home values, reduced commission rates and higher operating costs and the agent's net taxable income today would approximate $40,000 – **less than half** what the agent earned in 2006.

Tens of thousands of real estate agents have left the business. Many are sitting on the fence uncertain whether to continue.

Whether you are a brand-new agent or seasoned veteran looking to kick-start your career, know this: The real estate world has changed. Doing what your Uncle Harry did 25 years ago may not get you the results you want.

Identifying the many opportunities which exist in today's marketplace just might.

The marketing ideas presented in this book will help you know:

1) Where to find today's opportunities and,

2) How to pursue them effectively.

The world has changed.

Twenty years ago, we all knew how to find business. We advertised our listings in the real estate section of the Sunday classifieds, held open houses and cold-called neighborhoods to find listings. We solicited For-Sale-By-Owner (FSBO) homeowners and persuaded home sellers whose listing contracts had expired to change horses.

Cable real estate channels were the rage. They have all but disappeared today.

Cell phones were mounted to the floors of our cars and pagers were clipped to our belts. In the mid-90's, the internet was little more than a novelty.

In 1995, Mark Zuckerberg was 11 years old; Facebook didn't exist. Tweeting was something a canary did and Pinterest was a typo.

Less than 20 years later, Facebook has more than a billion participants worldwide. Pinterest is the fastest-growing social media site and Lady Gaga can Tweet to her 25 million monsters in a millisecond.

Today, more than 90% of home buyers begin their search on the internet.

Agents who are still doing business as they did 15 years ago are:

- **Comfortable.** They don't need more income. They are happy making the living they are now and have little motivation to increase it.

- **Complacent**. They are oblivious to changes in the marketplace and consumers' behavior. They do as they have always done.

- **Resistant to Change**. They are terrified to learn something new; many would rather quit the business than adapt to a changing market.

- **All of the above.**

If you have not read **"Who Moved My Cheese?"** by Dr. Spencer Johnson, buy it today. Then read it.

Chapter 2
Swim, sink, or get out of the water.

If you are considering starting a career in real estate – or ending one – you must ask yourself one question: *Are you willing to do what it takes to sell real estate today?*

The sink-or-swim method.

Most agents started into the business with a broker who tossed them into the deep end of the pool. They received almost no training and no marketing plan. Today, these agents are foundering, trying to find the success they once had by doing more of what they have always done.

> Insanity is doing the same thing
> over and over again
> expecting different results.
>
> ~Rita Mae Brown

Dive in headfirst or get out.

Getting a job in real estate is easy. You only need a real estate license, a half dozen signs, a stack of business cards, a computer, a cell phone and a marginally dependable car.

It is just as easy to get out of the business. There are plenty of agents to take your place. You will be missed for half an hour. Probably less.

If you are not willing to dive headlong into today's real estate environment, don't. Stop now before you spend any more money on Multiple Listing Service fees and yard signs. Today's top agents are tech-savvy and multi-dimensional. The best ones embrace old-school marketing – open houses and personal contact – as much as marketing via the internet, social media and e-mail bursts.

Today's top agents are highly mobile; they can write an offer with pen and paper on the hood of their car as easily as they can create electronic documents and get e-signatures on their iPad.

The choice is yours. Do it or don't. Your success is up to you.

You gotta' dance that Macarena.

A few years ago, I was conducting a seminar on internet marketing. After the program, a colleague asked, "Are you crazy? Your competitors were sitting in the audience. Why would you tell them what you do?"

"Because," I replied, "you can lead a horse to water but you can't make him dance the Macarena. I can tell this room full of 400 real estate agents exactly what to do to improve their business and fewer than five of them will actually go out and do what I told them." The ideas in this book will get your career on track … *if you actually do them.*

Chapter 3
Which way do you go?

Alice's Adventures in Wonderland

Alice, upon encountering the Cheshire Cat, asks, "Would you tell me, please, which way I ought to walk from here?"

"That depends a good deal on where you want to get to," said the Cat.
"I don't much care where –" said Alice.

"Then it doesn't matter which way you walk," said the Cat." – so long as I get somewhere," Alice added as an explanation.

"Oh, you're sure to do that," said the Cat, "if you only walk long enough."

Unless your plan is to walk aimlessly until you stumble into a paycheck, first determine which direction you want to go.

Countless times I've heard agents recall the day they passed the real estate exam. They showed up to the office bright and early the next morning, eager to start their real estate career. The broker pointed to a desk with a phone and a cross directory and instructed them, "Start calling." No training. No goal. No plan. They flailed about, hoping to connect with new clients.

Treat your career like a business.

Approach your real estate career as a business – one with a clear vision about who you are, what you do and how you intend to do it.

Open your eyes and your mind to all the possibilities in today's real estate arena. Some of what worked to make a living in real estate in 1995 still works; some doesn't.

That which doesn't, however, has been replaced with new opportunities if you know where to find them.

Build a business strategy which takes into account your personal strengths, the dynamics of your marketplace, competition, your broker, franchise affiliation and today's rapidly-changing consumer behavior.

Before you decide which path to take, do your homework.

Chapter 4
Measure twice, cut once.

Master carpenters make sure they place their saw in the right place by measuring twice and cutting once. Many real estate agents don't even own a ruler; they have no idea where to begin.

Before you plop yourself down at a desk and start dialing for dollars, 1) Measure yourself, your market and your competition and 2) Evaluate your prospective broker and franchise affiliation.

Learn as much as you can from experienced, successful agents in your office and in your marketplace. Pay attention to what they do. Notice where they spend their energy.

Measure yourself.

Honestly assess your personal strengths. Talk with your friends and family to get their perspectives about your personality and social style.

Are you outgoing or introverted? At parties, do you feel comfortable introducing yourself to strangers or do you wait for them to introduce themselves to you?

Do your friends say you have the gift of gab or are you more contemplative? Are you a problem-solver or problem-avoider?

Do people trust and like you? First and foremost, people do business with those they like and trust.

Some agents are successful pursuing business aggressively while others fail miserably at it. Conversely, those agents who have great success with their assertive style may land flat on their face in a highly social environment.

Tailor your strategy to your strengths. Don't try to be someone you're not because you believe it is what people expect of you. You will find the greatest satisfaction in your career if the way you do business reflects your values.

Measure your needs.

How many homes must you sell in a year to make a living? The answer depends on several factors:

1) *Your definition of "making a living."* What is your income goal? How much money do you feel you deserve to make each year? What do you need to meet your basic monthly financial obligations? What are your goals for personal and family needs, activities and interests – retirement savings, family vacations, music lessons, basketball camps, etc? How much money do you need in after-tax income to meet your financial goals?

2) *The prices of homes in your area.* If the average sales price of the homes in your market is $100,000, you may need to sell more homes to reach your income goal than an agent whose average sales price is higher. This is an important consideration in building a marketing strategy. Will you concentrate on selling more average-priced homes – which have more potential buyers – or more expensive homes which may be more challenging to sell?

3) *Your commission rate.* For purposes of illustration, let's say you charge a commission rate of 3% of a home's sales price. If you focus on average-priced homes, your average commission check will be about $3,000.

4) *Your costs of doing business.* Most agents earning $100,000 in gross commissions per year calculate their costs of doing business annually in the range of 30 – 40%. For every $3,000 commission check they receive, $900 – $1,200 of it goes out in advertising, computer expenses, cell phones, internet and MLS fees, fuel, automobile expense, etc.,

leaving a net income per transaction of about $2,000.

If you work in a moderately-priced market and your goal is $100,000 net income before taxes, you will need to sell 50 homes per year – about 4 per month.

Compare this number to your market's average number of homes sold per agent and you will see that selling 50 homes per year will probably rank you in the top 5% of all the agents in your area. You won't get there just showing up.

However, if your average sales price is higher, you will need to sell fewer homes to earn the same income. If the sales price is lower, however, you will need to sell more. Simple math.

Measure your market.

"Fish upstream," advises Dave Liniger, founder of RE/MAX International. That is, pre-empt your competition by getting to the prospects first. His advice assumes there are fish in the creek. Be certain there are.

> A blind pig can sometimes find
> truffles but it helps to know that
> they are found in oak forests.
>
> ~ David Ogilvy

Evaluate the size of your market – its population and housing turnover.

- How many people live in your subdivision, village or county?

- How many homes were listed on the Multiple Listing Service last year? How many of those listings expired unsold?

- How many homes sell in your market annually?

- What is the percentage of listings which actually sell?

- What is your market's average sales price, average time on the market and average actual sales price as a percent of list price?

- What is the average commission rate in your market? Commissions are negotiable and rates vary but your broker has the right to establish commission policies for his/her company.

- How many "For Sale by Owner" homes currently have signs in the front yard?

- How many Realtors are in your market? How many homes sell each year *per agent* in your market? (Calculate the annual number of homes sold on your MLS divided by the number of agents on your MLS)

Measure your broker.

Whether you are just starting out or currently associated with a broker, be smart. Your broker's investment in marketing will have a significant impact on your success. The same holds true of your broker's franchise affiliation … or lack thereof.

Choose your broker based on how he or she can help *you* – with training, technology, awareness, reputation and marketing support – not based on what you can do for *them*. Don't be penny-wise and pound-foolish. When you are getting started – or re-started – you need all the marketing support you can get.

- Does the broker provide training, leads and promotional materials to jump-start your business? Ask for a test drive of their support materials and lead-generating capabilities so you can make an informed comparison.

- Is the broker part of a national franchise? Starting out, riding the coattails of your broker's good reputation and top-of-mind awareness will give you a head start. If the broker is affiliated with a highly-recognized and respected franchise, you will reap the benefits.

- How much advertising does the broker and franchise do on a national and local level? Does the broker use only mass media or is he or she committed to social media marketing as well?

- How highly does the broker and franchise rank in consumers' awareness of real estate companies? Where do the franchise's and broker's web sites rank in the search engine results?

- Does the broker have an exceptional reputation within your community for integrity and leadership?

- Does he or she have the financial staying power to weather economic downturns and keep the lights on? Finding a new broker because yours went under will cause your business to falter – you will need to buy new yard signs, business cards and self-promotion. Most important, though, is that a sudden, unexpected change in your business identity will reflect negatively on your stability in the business.

- Does the broker embrace and support new technology and methods for getting business as well as the tried-and-true? Saving a few dollars each month on desk fees won't make up for the $5,000 commission you lose to a competitor who works for a powerhouse broker.

Give yourself the best chance for success. Once you have decided which broker will best help you jump-start your career, go there. Leave the one who isn't. No exceptions, no excuses.

Measure your competition.

- Who are the top agents in your market? Who do they work for? Working with the best will put money in your pocket.

- Which agents specialize in a particular neighborhood, school district or price range?

- Do you have the experience, knowledge and staying power to go up against established agents on their home turf? Can you realistically pre-empt them when they have home-court advantage? Are there other neighborhoods which may present better opportunities?

- Is your competition doing an effective job in social media marketing? Do agents have their own web sites and are they interactive with visitors?

- Do your competition's web sites have the capability to provide them with visitor contact information?

- Ask top agents what works in your marketplace and what does not. Learn what those agents do for business. They won't tell you all their secrets but they may tell you more than you expect. Ask several agents, not just the office's top producers.

Starting out in an office in Farmington Hills, Michigan, I watched what several high-level producers did to attract business. One called For Sale by Owners exclusively. Another distributed 7,000 monthly newsletters to three different subdivisions. Another concentrated on expired listings and still another held three open houses every weekend. Each had their own way of doing business – the one which worked for them. But they shared one thing in common: They all focused on *listing homes.*

Chapter 5
Make seven promises.

Before moving on to strategies and techniques, make yourself seven promises.

1. Commit to list, not sell.

This is mentioned first because it is the most important. Whether you are in a buyer's market or seller's market, working with 20 sellers is more efficient – and profitable – than working with 20 buyers.

Don't worry. You will get your chance to work with buyers. Many of those homeowners whose houses you sell will need another place to live – just don't spend your time looking for them. Spend your time getting and selling listings.

2. Set goals. Real goals.

"World peace" is not a goal. It is an aspiration. If your goal is "to gain financial security," try again. "Putting my kids through college" is not a real goal; it is a dream.

Real goals are specific and more. Although "Earning $100,000" is specific, it still does not qualify as a real goal. Real goals are achievements you *truly* want. If you are not motivated by money, making $100,000 is not a motivating goal.

If your dream is to buy a nicer home for your family, shop for the type of home you desire. How much does it cost? How many bedrooms and baths? What neighborhood? Which schools?

When do you want it? Creating a deadline for achieving your goal will help you identify what you must to do to get it.

Be careful of falling into the trap of thinking of only materialistic goals. What do you want in your life – personally as well as professionally?

Write down your goal and tape it to a picture of your goal. Tape them both to your computer screen so you see them every day. Remind yourself why you are there.

3. Be big somewhere.

As a marketing strategist for J. Walter Thompson (JWT), I told my clients: "Be big somewhere. Pick a market and own it. It is better to be the big fish in a small pond than it is to be a medium-sized fish in the ocean. Nobody notices medium-sized fish but they cannot ignore the fish who owns the pond."

Too often, real estate agents try to be everything to everyone and they wind up scurrying about like a man with a paper backside running through a forest fire. Their career controls them, not the other way around.

"Be big somewhere" describes niche marketing. When you focus on your niche – the one thing you do better than anyone else – and do it over and over and over again, chances are you will be successful.

Once you choose your niche – *prospect relentlessly.*

4. Prospect relentlessly.

In his seminars, Floyd Wickman, the renowned real estate trainer, tells the story of Domenico Siciliano, an immigrant who could barely speak – or understand – English. He repeatedly failed the real estate license exam. He eventually passed the test and Floyd sat him down at a desk with a black, rotary-dial telephone and the three inch-thick White Pages. Floyd predicted poor Domenico would give up after only a few days.

Call after call, Domenico introduced himself, "Hello? My name is Domenico Siciliano. I sell da' houses. You wan' me to come over … or *WHAT?"*

Startled and confused, many homeowners asked, *"What?"*

Without missing a beat, Domenico jumped from his chair and yelled, "I'll be right there!!" The homeowner's head was still spinning as Domenico charged out the door.

Domenico was relentless in his prospecting and tenacious in his pursuit of new clients. He knew that every time someone hung up on him or turned him away when he knocked on their door, he was that much closer to getting a listing.

Whatever pond you choose to fish, you must *prospect relentlessly.*

5. Protect your time.

It's your job to value your time because nobody else will. Be prudent with your time. Spend your work day doing what makes you money, not organizing office parties or chit-chatting over the water cooler about the weekend football scores.

Treat your job as if you have a boss looking over your shoulder. You do; it is *you.*

6. Schedule your activities.

Schedule your work week in advance. Use a calendar you can keep in front of you on your desk. At the end of each week, schedule your most important activities for the next week – blocks of time for prospecting, listing appointments, showing homes, posting in social media, working floor time, updating your database, and so on.

Prospecting is the most important. It is more important than going to closings or listing appointments. Successful agents may not have a closing every week or get a new listing but they always make time to prospect … week in, week out. Year in, year out.

Prospecting is like wetlands – it is so important that if you need to move it, you must replace it somewhere else in your work week. Without fail.

Include your personal responsibilities on the same calendar – Kids' soccer games, Parent-Teacher conferences, time for your relationship, exercise, etc. Maintain balance. If you are working less than 40 hours a week, you have a part-time job. Working 60 hours a week will eventually take a toll on your health, your personal life and family responsibilities.

7. Keep showing up. No matter what.

Nobody understands the emotional roller coaster a real estate career can be better than I do – victory, elation, failure, desperation, and success. Not necessarily in that order.

Expect it. You will not land every listing appointment. You will not sell every listing – even saleable ones. Deals will fall through just when you need them the most. Buyers you have invested time with will buy a home from another agent. Sellers who promised to list with you don't. Closings will be delayed. Banks and other agents will cause nightmares. Just when nothing more could go wrong, it does.

Despite doing everything you should be doing, you hit the wall. There will be times your career is hell.

> When you're going
> through hell,
> keep going.
>
> ~ Winston Churchill

Believe in yourself. Believe in your abilities. Keep showing up. Every day.

Chapter 6
Where will you fish?

Once you have decided which broker and franchise to join, you have set goals, and you know a bit about your market and your competition, what next?

> If you give a man a fish
> he will eat for a day.
> If you teach a man to fish
> he will eat for a lifetime.
>
> ~ English Proverb

You need to pick your fishin' hole. How do you decide which pond is right for you? If your market size is small, you may need to do all of them. In larger markets, you may do well to carve your niche in a segment of the market and own it.

Consider the various prospecting methods. Historically, there were two types of prospecting – 1) passive and 2) active. Today, the lines are blurred because of the advent of social media.

Passive Prospecting

Think of them this way: If you work in a men's store at the mall, your job is to stand in the store waiting for a customer to walk in and buy a shirt. It is passive prospecting.

Active Prospecting

If, on the other hand, you pick up the phone and call someone to ask him if he needs new clothes and to tell him about your new stock of shirts and ties, that is active marketing.

Social Media Marketing.

Marketing via social media is a hybrid of sorts. Like passive marketing, it will help you build awareness with the public about your knowledge level and the services you offer. It is active because you are interacting with clients, prospects and peers daily albeit not often directly.

What is right for you?

As you read the next several chapters, ask yourself what feels right – What fits you? Again, if you are in a limited market, you may not have the luxury to choose one prospecting style or strategy; you may need to participate in several of them.

No matter what prospecting methods you choose, you must:

- Create immediate and broad awareness with the public that you are in the real estate business,

- Build synergism in your marketing communications,

- Engage with potential customers and

- Uncover opportunities to do business.

Part II
Prospect Relentlessly

■■■■■■■■■■■■■■■■■■■■■■■■■■■■■■■■■

Chapter 7
Spread the word.

Passive marketing builds top-of-mind awareness; it does not ask for the order. But starting by getting the word out is essential. Over time, more and more people will think of you first when they think about real estate. Just don't expect overnight results.

Build synergism with your marketing communications.

Synergism in marketing communications is the principle that the cumulative awareness achieved is greater than the sum of its parts. If you see 5 television commercials from a fast food restaurant in an hour, for example, your brain may believe you saw 8.

Getting started more than 25 years ago, I noticed that other agents placed 6-inch sign riders atop their real estate yard signs with their names and phone numbers printed on them. The letters were 2" high and completely unreadable from the street. Except in the rare case when a driver stopped, parked and walked up to the sign with pen and paper, the signs were utterly useless.

I ordered sign riders printed with my name only – in 4" letters. They were easily visible from a car doing 40 down the road. Then I canvassed up and down the busiest streets of the city looking for listings. Nobody else wanted those listings because they were nearly impossible to sell. It didn't matter; I wasn't looking for sales. My goal was to build name awareness.

Before long, friends were telling me they saw my signs and how impressed they were with how many listings I had. I didn't; I never had more than 6 at the time. Nevertheless, because the listings were on busy streets, they saw them frequently and assumed I had other listings on non-busy streets, too.

To build top-of-mind awareness, promote your name everywhere – Facebook, Twitter, Pinterest, LinkedIn, the internet, yard signs, open houses and more. Create an e-mail signature with all your contact information – name, phone number, e-mail address, postal address, web site URL and hyperlink to "find me on Facebook." Use it for all e-mail communications – replies, forwards and new e-mails.

Use a contact management system.

Keep track of your contact with your database – your past clients and friends and family to whom you have mailed promotional materials or spoken with in

38

person or by telephone or communicated with via e-mail. Write everything down and keep it.

Rolf Anderson, internationally-renowned real estate and technology trainer, once said, "The best technology is the technology you use." A "contact management system" can be as technologically simple as 3 x 5 recipe cards held together with an alligator paper clip if it works for you. Spiral-bound notebooks fit nicely into a briefcase – they are about the same size as an iPad.

Contact management systems can be as advanced as software designed to maintain your database, store complete contact information – including names, addresses, phone numbers, e-mail addresses, birthdays, anniversaries, names of your contacts' children, the date they moved into the home they bought from you, etc. There are several good contact management systems available: Top Producer, Constant Contact, RealtyJuggler, Sage ACT!, ContactPlus and others.

Use what works for *you*.

Knowing when you sent your last mailing will help you maintain ongoing contact with your database at regular intervals. Knowing when you spoke with them and what you talked about makes you look smart.

Passive prospecting includes telling your friends and family, business and personal networking, farming, ranching, internet and electronic marketing, working floor time, holding open houses and simply meeting people.

1. Tell your friends, family, past clients and more.

Your family, friends, neighbors, past clients and business associates are good long-term prospects for business. Working with people who like you and respect you is the best possible business.

Past clients remember if you did a good job when they worked with you and are likely to refer you to their friends and family. When it's time for them to move again, there's a good chance they will call you, particularly if you have kept your name in front of them.

Treat your insurance agent as your friend and he or she will probably reciprocate your friendship and your business.

Create your Friends and Family mailing list. Mail something to them every month and call them every quarter no matter what other marketing tactics you employ. Ask for their e-mail addresses and ask them if you may include them in your e-mail database.

Building this foundation of your real estate business is not optional. Do this first before anything else. As your Friends and Family list grows with past clients and their referrals, your friends, family and business peers will provide a base of business which will sustain you through even the toughest markets.

Starting out, though, your Friends and Family list will probably not provide enough business to pay your bills. Unless you are independently wealthy or plan to rely on a spouse's income, you will need to combine this with other prospecting methods to get started.

2. Get Belly-to-Belly.

Many highly-successful salespeople are naturally gregarious. They thrive on social engagement. They have done social networking for decades – long before Twitter or Facebook. They do it face-to-face, handshake-to-handshake, eyeball-to-eyeball.

Get up from your desk, leave your office and get social. Meet people. Talk with them. Get to know them. Remember:

> Nobody cares how much you know until they know how much you care.
>
> ~ Theodore Roosevelt

Jerry is a financial planner and friend I have known for nearly 40 years. As I was doing research for this book, I asked him how he prospects for business. "I go to dinner."

"You go to dinner?" I asked, "You're saying you take prospects out to dinner?"

"No, I go alone. I pick a different restaurant every night. There are always people to talk to; they love to talk about their family, their jobs, anything. I am there to listen. Sometimes they ask what I do; sometimes they don't. But often enough, they have my business card in their hand when they leave. Even if they don't, I've had a great dinner and good conversation."

So, each day, he leaves his office mid-afternoon. His co-workers laugh and ask, "Going prospecting, are you?'

He smiles and replies, "Yep" and then decides which restaurant sounds good today.

Jeff is a Hall of Fame Realtor with RE/MAX, my co-worker and friend for more than 20 years. He prospects the same way Jerry does. He calls it "Going golfing."

As he walked past our new receptionist one mid-January afternoon with a Michigan blizzard rolling in, she asked "Are you out for the day?"

"Yep. Going golfing."

She figured it out one rainy day in April.

Be in the *people* business first, the real estate business second.

3. Network. Volunteer.

Numerous business networking groups have been created expressly for the purpose of establishing business relationships, such as the Michigan Business and Professional Organization, BNI International and Toastmasters.

Service organizations such as the Lions Club, Rotary Club and your local business-development council are excellent places to interact with people in your community.

Fraternal organizations like the B.P.O.E. and Shriners International are examples of pre-internet social networking dating back to the 1800's.

Volunteer to help your school's athletic and band boosters, coach a Little League team or lead a Boy Scout or Girl Scout Troup. If the other parents like and respect you, there's a good chance they will do business with you. The bonus of getting to spend time with your kids is worth all the money in the world.

4. Farming

Some agents start by "farming." Just like it sounds, agents cordon off an area – a neighborhood, for example – and cultivate the residents' awareness of them as the neighborhood expert. Farming Realtors® regularly contact their farm through monthly newsletters announcing neighborhood news, items for sale, new babies and new listings. They knock on doors and visit every garage sale in the subdivision. They spearhead neighborhood events like block parties and neighborhood garage sales.

Farming is an excellent strategy for building long-term business. It is a socially-interactive strategy which showcases your neighborhood involvement and expertise. It is a particularly effective strategy when combined with today's social media marketing.

Just as it takes time for a vineyard to grow and produce fruit, *farming takes considerable time to reap your harvest.*

5. Ranching

Ranching is farming on steroids. Typical real estate farms will range in size from 100 homes to 500 homes. Smart agents who know the importance of consistent contact have expanded their farms into ranches – considerably larger versions of farms. Often, ranches may include 5,000 or 10,000 homes receiving monthly newsletters, open house invitations, and "just listed" or "just sold" announcements. Successful ranching agents may send 2 – 4 mailings per month to their database.

Do the math: Sending two mailings per month to 5,000 homes = 120,000 pieces of mail per year. At today's postcard rate it adds up to about $35,000 for postage alone. On average, there is a 10% turnover rate in real estate; that is, 500 of those homes will go up for sale in any give year. As the agent whose name pops into their heads first, there's a good chance you will be the one they call. Even if you only get 20% market share, you will list 100 homes per year from your ranch alone. If the average commission on those sales is $3,000,

45

working a 5,000-home ranch could generate $300,000 per year income all by itself.

Ranching is highly effective but it is also very expensive and should only be done by agents who have the financial resources to commit to ranching for a minimum of three years.

6. Internet web site marketing.

If you don't already have your own personal real estate web site, do not bother creating own now. That train has left the station. Consumers click on only the top non-sponsored search results before they get bored and move on. If your site does not appear on the first page of non-sponsored search results, it won't be seen.

Unless you have extremely deep pockets or a middle-schooler gifted in search engine optimization, your chance of building a web site today which rises to the top of the search results is between zero and none. Closer to zero. There are plenty of webmasters out there who might say differently but ask them for a money-back guarantee if you don't get in the top three of the non-sponsored search results. Let me know how that works out.

This does not apply, however, to a well-established local broker's site or a national-franchise site. **Participating in lead-generating, interactive sites provided by**

your broker or franchise is worth every penny you pay in advertising or franchise fees.

7. Use electronic marketing.

E-mail marketing pays off. The Direct Marketing Association estimates that for $1 invested in e-mail marketing, it returns $40 in revenue (Source: The Magill Report.) E-mail marketing is most effective when you have important and worthwhile information to share with your electronic database, particularly when your database includes a high percentage of friends and family and people who have visited your web site, your company's web site or have inquired about a home via e-mail.

Purchase a professionally-designed e-mail marketing program to announce new listings, open houses, price reductions and to distribute a monthly e-newsletter packed with market trends and real estate updates. Most contact management software systems include e-mail marketing packages.

Expand your electronic marketing beyond consumers. Build a separate database which includes the top Realtors in your MLS. According to the National Association of Realtors, the top 5% of agents in any geographic market do 95% of the business. When you merchandise your new listings to the top agents in your market, you will reach 95% of the buyers looking for homes with

Realtors. When you have built a reputation with those agents as someone who lists homes to sell, they will be eager to show your listings before other agents get around to it.

Be careful with e-mail marketing, however. Know and abide by regulations regarding e-mail spam; spam is annoying and counter-productive. It has the potential to do more harm than good. Done sparingly, however, it will position you as a Realtor who is aggressively marketing his clients' homes.

8. Work floor time.

"Floor time" is the practice of scheduling licensed agents to be present in the office for a block of time to field questions about listings and meet with walk-in clients.

Floor time is passive prospecting. You sit at your desk waiting for the phone to ring or someone to walk in the door.

Nevertheless, some agents are gifted in the art of turning a floor call into a sale. The best ones are effective counter-punchers.

The most successful floor time agentr\e those who do more than answer questions. They have the ability to shift into active prospecting mode by countering a potential client's questions with their own.
When a caller requests information ("What's the price of the house on Hickory Street?"),

the agent provides the answer ("$249,900")
… and asks a question of his own ("Are you
looking for homes in that area?") Highly-
successful floor salespeople use the
customer's inquiry about a property to
establish dialogue and glean information
helpful in finding the customer the home
which is right for them.

Some of the great boxers in history were
remarkable counter-punchers. Learn this
sweet science, do it relentlessly and it will
pay dividends.

With today's call-forwarding technology,
some real estate offices have eliminated
floor time altogether. If your personal
marketing strategy includes floor time, be
sure you are affiliated with an office which
offers it.

9. Hold open houses.

Highly social people do well holding open
houses. If you make friends easily, holding
open houses is an excellent way to jump into
your career with both feet. Hold as many as
you can – two or three every weekend
depending on customs in your market. It
doesn't matter whether it is your listing or
not. Ask agents in your office if you can
hold open houses on their listings.

Starting out, your objective is to meet
people. You will be surprised how many
people you will meet again and again. They

will think you are a skilled pro and hard worker – just the kind they want when they sell their home.

Find the agents in your company who are the most successful holding open houses and ask to attend their open houses. Watch what they do. While each may have his or her own style, they have common practices:

1) **They are always prepared.** Take more business cards and "Open House" brochures than you need. Take several blank purchase agreements. You never know when two or three buyers will have serious interest in the home you are showcasing.

2) **They "Pre-Market" the Open House.** Walk the neighborhood handing out flyers announcing a "Neighbors Only" Open House the morning before the public open house. Mail postcards to the neighborhood, place "Open Sunday" signs at least 4 days prior to the open.

   Announce it on your MLS, send e-bursts, Tweets and post it on Facebook.

3) **They use plenty of directional "Open House" signs.** Use 8 or 10 signs to guide potential customers

from major thoroughfares to the home.

4) **They turn on all the lights.** Open all the window coverings. Dark corners repel visitors. Let the light shine in.

5) **They ask the homeowner to bake a pie**, cookies or home-made bread beforehand. Odors are the quickest offenders to a good first impression. Make the house smell like a home.

6) **They use a sign-in sheet** when appropriate. In some markets, visitors understand the importance of knowing who has been in the Seller's home and they will sign willingly. In other areas, sign-in sheets are off-putting.

7) **They use "Fair Trades."** An alternative to sign-in sheets to capture contact information from visitors is offering them information on financing, comparable homes, information on their home's value, etc.

The key to this strategy is to avoid simply giving away the information but to offer to send it via e-mail or postal mail.

8) **They always greet each visitor with a smile**, a handshake and a brochure.

Assure them you are there to help with any questions but whatever you do, do not follow them around the house like a yappy dog. Be cordial and welcoming, not high-pressure.

If your marketing plan is to focus your energies solely and relentlessly on these passive marketing methods, they will pay off ... eventually.

Chapter 8
Commit to social media marketing.

I am flabbergasted by the percentage of Realtors who are not yet actively engaged in social networking, or as it is better known today, social media marketing. Many have never visited Facebook, LinkedIn, Twitter or Pinterest, even though a huge percentage of their potential clients are actively engaged in these social media sites every day of their lives.

Social media marketing presents the greatest emerging growth opportunity for the real estate business.

Look at the numbers.

In the United States, Generation Y (ages 17 – 32) totals 72 million people. The Baby Boom generation (ages 48 – 66) has a population of 55 million. Today's Gen Y is 31% *larger* than the Baby Boomers.

Many corporate CEOs and Marketing veeps still believe the Baby Boom generation is the largest, most-consuming generation of all. It is not. Gen Y is today's largest generation by far and enjoys a comparatively high level of disposable income.

As important, Gen Y is in the prime first-time-homebuyer age range. They are prospects for homes, paint, carpeting, appliances, minivans, furniture and more. If they are married with children, most have dual incomes. Traditionally, first-time home buyers make up one-third to one-half of all home buyers in the market at any given time.

66% of Generation Y will visit an online store if they see their friends have visited it. That's 2/3 of the market – nearly 50 million people. On average, they have 700 Facebook friends as compared the overall population's average of 140.

Stop. Let that sink in. 72 Million potential real estate purchasers have an average of 700 friends each. (Source: Meet Generation C, the Connected Consumer, by Brian Solis) Social media connections represent an enormous market for new business.

It's as much about what they do as who they are.

Most important, though, is how Gen Y'ers communicate, socialize and experience entertainment. Unlike Boomers who had to get to the couch by 8:00 p.m. on Tuesday night to catch Laverne & Shirley, Gen Y'ers watch their favorite programs on their schedule by recording it, saving it on U-Verse or Tivo or watching it online via Hulu. They are not slaves to prime-time programming as Baby Boomers were.

Where are they spending their time? They are Playing Words with Friends and interacting with friends on Facebook. They are playing video games or uploading videos to YouTube. Baby Boomers leafed through the Sears Roebuck catalog dreaming of the things they'd buy someday. Gen Y is shopping online and posting their favorite picks to Pinterest.

In the past five years, social media has gone nuclear – from 2005 to 2011, the minutes spent in social media networks and blogs multiplied 12 times. 64% of mobile web time is spent on apps – today's consumer is not constrained to their desktop computer or laptop to access information immediately.

The demand for information is not limited to Generation Y. 89% of Americans have access to the internet and more than half of them spend 3 or more hours a week on social media sites like Facebook, Pinterest, Tumblr and others.

If you know where 89% of your market is and you're not there, you probably should ask yourself if you are serious about your business.

Today, tech-savvy Realtors are building business through social media marketing, particularly in conjunction with other prospecting methods. Through social networking, Realtors can stay in frequent contact with their friends, family and past clients (and their friends) on Facebook, followers on Twitter and professional connections and career-related groups on LinkedIn.

Pursuing business through social media must be done prudently. You must remain sensitive to the forums in which you engage. Spamming your Facebook personal page with real estate pitches, announcements of new listings, price reductions and open houses will irritate more people than those who will find your posts worthwhile.

Starting out, keep your social media marketing strategy simple.

1. **Facebook**

    A) **Create a Facebook Personal Timeline**

        As you build your Facebook "friends" list, post daily to your personal Facebook page. Share an interesting story or join in a discussion but be careful your posts are not too frequently real estate–related.

        Visitors to Facebook are there to interact *socially* – to exchange news about their families, to share a funny story or post pictures of events in their lives. Be sincere in your interest and let them know who you are as a person. You may be surprised how many common interests you share once you connect with them personally.

If you appear to be constantly drumming up real estate business you will appear superficial and only interested in their business, not in their lives.

Search Facebook for all of your past clients and customers, neighbors and those with whom you do business. Friend them. If they choose to accept your friend request, Facebook is great way to keep your name uppermost in their minds.

B) **Create a Facebook Business Page.**

It is completely acceptable to talk real estate on your Facebook business page. Create a business page and post new listings, price reductions, recent sales and more. Post pictures of the "SOLD" sign on your listings or a photo of you handing a new home buyer their house keys. Ask your clients for testimonials and their permission to post them on your Facebook Business Page. Make sure your Facebook business page has your contact information including your cell phone and e-mail address.

Upload virtual tours and informational videos about the process of buying or selling, market trends and more. Most national franchises have professionally-produced videos available to upload to your Facebook business page.

On Facebook, news is old within hours – sometimes minutes. Be certain the information you are providing is current and *compelling*.

The better the information you share, the more your page visitors will see you as their real estate resource.

C) **Create Facebook Events.**

Create a Facebook event for every open house and invite your Facebook friends to attend the event. Whether you are posting to your personal Facebook page or your Facebook business page, remember to keep the "social" in social media marketing.

D) **Promote your Facebook business page.**

Improve your ranking and reach on Facebook by inviting your personal Facebook friends and agents in other markets to "like" your business page.

Before you know it, you will have created your own referral network.

As importantly, once you have received 30 "likes" for your business page, Facebook provides you with analytics – tracking reports on your page's activity. Pay attention to the analytics. Notice which posts result in high readership and traffic. Do more of them.

E) **Join real estate groups on Facebook.**

Your local Realtor association may have one and there are several groups created as a clearing house for referrals. Don't be afraid to start one yourself.

2. **Pinterest**

The fastest-growing social media web site today, Pinterest has an audience skewed heavily female. It is the mother lode for real estate and home-improvement marketers. Why? Because, according to Forbes, women initiate 80% of all home-improvement purchases, from kitchens and bathrooms to flooring and window coverings.

In 31% of American households, a woman makes the family's real estate decisions. But the "initiating decision" is heavily skewed female. Some studies show that the woman in the family initiates the home-shopping process as much as 75% of the time. If your marketing fails to target women, you are missing out … big-time.

Pinning your listings on Pinterest will merchandise your clients' homes to the primary *influencer* of a family's real estate purchases.

3. **Twitter**

According to the Pew Research Center, in the 14 months from November 2010 to February 2012, Twitter usage on a daily basis quadrupled from 2% of adults to 8%. Although Twitter's users currently skew younger, it is important to look to the future. Twitter adult users tend to be from higher incomes and educations. Twitter's growth is expected to outpace most other social media as smart phones saturate the market, particularly with consumers in higher income and education segments.

Twitter's 140- character format is not an ideal platform for sharing lengthy real estate ads but it will help you build top-of-mind awareness with your friends, associates and referring agents across the country.

If you have a considerable following of consumers and other Realtors, your "new listing" tweet might land you a quick sale or instant referral.

Sharing links to a real estate-related article or your blog will build your reputation as a knowledgeable Realtor abreast with current real estate trends.

4 LinkedIn

LinkedIn is a career networking site connecting professionals with business relationships for the purpose of networking.

LinkedIn members' ages, disposable incomes and education levels trend higher than other social media alternatives. If you want to pursue higher-end sales, join LinkedIn, create your profile and post articles about real estate, business and the economy.

Invite co-workers, peers and professionals to connect with you on LinkedIn. Join LinkedIn real estate groups like NAR and Realtor®. Share articles with other Realtors and career professionals locally and nationally.

Cross-pollinate your LinkedIn connections to follow you on Twitter and like your Facebook business page. Synergism.

5. **Blogging**

More than ten years after it began, most people still don't know what blogging is. Think newspaper. For decades, newspapers have featured an editorial page where the editor shares his or her opinion on a topic.

"Blogging" is the Op-Ed (Opinion-Editorial) page in the world of social media; it is your blank canvas to share information with your followers. Blogging is an excellent way to build your reputation as a knowledgeable Realtor. Blogging can be time-consuming, though, so keep your articles short. Re-post interesting articles from real estate experts from across the country but be sure to give journalistic credit to the author.

Create your blog and write brief articles – 1 or 2 paragraphs – on real estate. Find and re-post articles from recognized experts. There are several sites which provide free blogs, including Google and Wordpress.

Encourage your readers to comment on your blog posts and share the link on Facebook, LinkedIn and Twitter. Your Twitter followers or Facebook friends may be thinking of making a move now! You will also connect with Realtors from other markets who are tuning in to your blog. When they have a client moving to your area, they will think of you first to send a referral.

Join public blog sites like ActiveRain or Knoji.com and post articles of interest. Other Realtors and potential customers across the country will read your posts and perceive you as a real estate expert.

6. **RSS Publishing**

Create your own Electronic Real Estate Daily Newspaper featuring real estate articles as well as stories of local interest – sports, local political issues and human interest stories. Once the electronic feeds are established, the paper constructs and distributes itself daily to your Twitter followers and Facebook friends. It is a low-maintenance alternative to blogging.

Generations X and Y will increasingly saturate social media. Baby Boomers and even Greatest Generation grandmas and grandpas increasingly log on every day to interact with their children and grandchildren.

As your business grows, hire a social media expert like Ace Marketing/Events LLC or H3 Designs to develop and implement a more comprehensive social media marketing strategy.

Chapter 9
Beat the bushes.

Most agents who get a real estate license start out on a shoestring. They need business *fast* and cannot afford to wait for passive marketing or social media to pay off.

Nothing is more effective than active prospecting to generate business quickly.

As its name suggests, active prospecting is direct contact initiated for the expressed purpose of getting business. Whether you are blindly calling telephone numbers or targeting your calls to FSBOs (For Sale by Owners), responding to internet leads, knocking on doors or soliciting expired listings, active prospecting is the most difficult – albeit the most successful – method of gaining clients quickly.

Mike Littlejohn, a successful RE/MAX agent in Kansas City, Missouri, says "If you talk to enough people, you can throw up on every third one and still make a living." Mike's graphic message is clear: Talk to enough people and losing a few of them along the way won't stop you from making a living. You don't need to be perfect if you hit the numbers and prospect relentlessly.

1. **Cold Calling**

    Every experienced salesperson knows selling is a game of numbers.

Like many agents with no plan, I began by cold-calling. I pored over cross directories and phone books, phoning up and down the street looking for someone who might be thinking about making a move.

"Start at the back of the book," the pros suggest, "those poor bastards never hear from anyone. By the time new agents get halfway through the book, they quit."

Cold-calling. Good name. They were right. I quit after three pages.

2. Door knocking

Amazingly, some brokers are still telling new agents to start by knocking on doors. That's right: Walking through neighborhoods knocking on doors and ringing doorbells.

Imagine selling real estate before telephones. A real estate agent climbed onto his buckboard wagon and went from farm to farm, knocking on every farmhouse door. When the farmer answered, the agent asked,

"You wanna' sell your farm?"

"Nope."

So the real estate agent climbed back up onto the buckboard and clip-clopped off to the next farm.

We have telephones today. We have internet sites and cell phones and e-mail and facsimile machines. There is a reason we don't have horses and buggies any more. We have tools and technology to do business more efficiently.

Time is not money. Time is life.

Time is life. Remember this before you decide to cold call or walk through neighborhoods ringing doorbells. Remember this before you make an appointment with a homeowner who is unrealistic about the price he wants for his home or put a home buyer in your car that is not pre-qualified and motivated to buy now.

Don't give up that piece of your life; you cannot get it back. You can lose money and replace it. You can never replace time. Your time is your life. Time is more valuable than money.

Making a living in real estate depends on your ability to do as much business possible in the least amount of time. To increase your effectiveness and generate income faster, you must raise your skill level to identify the best prospects quickly.

Spend your time on warm leads.

If time is life, spend your time – your life –
wisely. Concentrate on those prospects
most likely to put a check in your pocket.
Focus on warm leads rather than cold
prospecting.

Warm leads are people you have reason to
believe want to buy or sell real estate.
Warm leads include "come list me" calls,
office walk-ins, internet web sites, For Sale
by Owners and expired listings.

3. Internet leads

Internet leads are the most plentiful but
lowest-quality warm leads. Until you
contact the web site visitor in person or
by e-mail, you don't know if they are
just curious to know the price of a house
in their neighborhood or they need to
buy and close in two weeks.

Respond to internet leads FAST.

Put yourself in the consumer's chair and
mind. They are cruising the internet
because they want information now –
right now. They expect immediate
gratification. For the most success with
internet leads, respond immediately –
preferably within 10 minutes by phone,
text or e-mail.

With internet leads, take the "How can I help?" approach. Some will be standoffish and want to retain their anonymity. Others more familiar with the internet may be ready to talk with you immediately.

Dance their dance. Let them lead. Accept that you will receive their trust only as quickly as they are willing to give it.

That said, learn to qualify and categorize internet leads according to their motivation, urgency and financial ability to buy or sell.

Four sources of internet leads are:

a) **Personal Real Estate Web Site**

If you already have your own personal web site for real estate, position your contact information at the top. Don't make your web site visitors search for it. Make it easy for them to call, e-mail or text you.

Provide as much information as possible on your listings, how-to articles on buying and selling, good resources for financing, fix-up hints, staging resources and school districts.

Offer some information freely but remember: Your web site is not a library. It is not a public service. It exists to get you business. You are paying good money to provide valuable information and you deserve something in return – their contact information.

Install a gateway to listing details. A gateway is a pop-up screen which asks for name, address, phone number and e-mail address and automatically and instantly e-mails their information to you.

You may need to ask your webmaster for help but it is worth the effort.

b) **Local Broker Web Sites**

Some forward-thinking local brokers jumped into internet explosion early and still maintain web sites which continue to draw visitors. Conduct your own Google search for "real estate" in your city and state ("Grand Rapids MI real estate," for example) and see yourself where your prospective company ranks.

If your broker's web site is not on the first page of non-sponsored search results – preferably at the top – the chances the company's web site will put money in your pocket is slim.

If the broker site ranks high, be sure the company uses the web site to capture leads and distribute them to its real estate agents. If they don't, find a company which does.

Instead of building your own personal web site from scratch, put your energy into creating a rock 'em, sock 'em business page on Facebook. Treat it as your personal web site.

c) National-Franchise Web Sites

The lead-generating power of the internet is no more evident than with national real estate franchises' web sites. Most of the big guns have them. National franchises offer value in the brand awareness, training, information and marketing power they give their agents. The lead-capture capabilities of the franchise sites are technologically sophisticated; they have the ability to forward information about their web site visitors to their agents within milliseconds after consumers log on.

Over the past few years, many local and regional companies gained considerable ground on big franchises in what they offer agents in lead generation, lead capture, and consistent contact with your database.

National franchises continue to hold an advantage in their referral networks. National franchises encourage referral sharing to other agents and brokers who share the same brand.

An agent in Des Moines who has a seller moving to San Diego can earn a referral fee by finding a San Diego agent to help his client buy a home.

Before choosing a broker, be sure to evaluate its online presence, its lead-generating capabilities and the number of offices throughout the country where you might exchange referrals.

d) Subscription Lead-Generation Web Sites

There are many independent, third-party real estate web sites which collect visitors' contact information. These web sites will happily sell leads to you. Some collect a referral fee but most require you pay up-front subscription fees. As with most internet leads, they vary in quality.

Before you pay for an independent lead-generation site, ask agents who have used them for references and recommendations.

Realtor.com
TheRedX
Homes.com
Zillow
Trulia

Chapter 10
Soft-sell FSBOs.

Drive down any street and you will see black & white signs in front yards – For Sale by Owner. FSBOs are warm leads. You know they want to sell. You should also know:

- FSBOs don't want to pay a real estate commission. They often perceive paying a commission as wasting money.

- FSBOs believe they are the most capable to sell their own home; they know its features more thoroughly than any agent could.

- FSBOs place little value in the level of exposure the Multiple Listing Service can give them.

- FSBOs rarely consider the legal ramifications of selling their own homes. Very few are real estate experts. Even though FSBO sales make up just 10% of all real estate sales, they account for 50% of all real estate lawsuits. (Source: National Association or Realtors.)

Understanding your prospect's mind is essential to deciding whether this is the right fishin' hole for you.

Realtors who have worked FSBOs successfully acknowledge three things:

1) Converting a FSBO to a listing requires patience and a slow-sell approach. Provide information, stay in touch every week. Stop in to see their home when they have an open house but don't hang around – get in and get out. They don't want you there while they are presenting their home to potential buyers.

2) Understand you will be investing a lot of time pursuing prospects who may eventually list with a friend or relative they had in mind before they decided to sell by owner.

3) The length of time it takes for a FSBO to change his mind is unpredictable; it varies with every seller. It is subject to change without notice. A FSBO may tell you they are not going to list with ANY Realtor for at least three months only to change their mind after they sat for four hours in an open house where nobody showed up. Or they may still be slogging it out 18 months later.

If you choose to pursue For Sale by Owner properties, remember:

1) Buyers who shop FSBOs do so for one reason: They believe they can

negotiate a lower price since the seller is not paying a commission.

There's the rub: Both the FSBO seller and the FSBO buyer expect to save the commission. They both believe that cutting out the middleman will save them money. If a seller has only one house to sell but the buyer is considering many homes, which one is more likely to save the commission? The buyer.

2) You can give their home more exposure. Greater exposure means more competition and more competition means better offers.

Through the MLS and co-operative agreements with third-party real estate web sites, you can provide exposure on every major real estate web site – from your local Realtor association web site to Realtor.com, RE/MAX, Coldwell Banker, Prudential, Century 21 – even Zillow and Trulia.

3) You can bring a sales force of thousands of commission-hungry co-operating Realtors who want to get a paycheck by selling their home.

4) You can help them avoid misunderstandings between buyer and seller with clearly-written purchase agreements which will reduce their

likelihood of winding up in court. (Always recommend they consult an attorney to review their purchase agreement. It's cheaper than hiring one later.)

Despite all these facts, remember this:

You will not change a FSBO's mind.

Only THEY can change their minds and many of them won't. Many will accept lower offers than you could have gotten them (even after commission) because they have convinced themselves a Realtor would have cut the price, too.

Only time will cause them to change their minds. After they have marketed the home themselves unsuccessfully for several months – and the property is now "market weary" – they will probably list it with a Realtor. In fact, 8 out of 10 FSBOs eventually list with a Realtor. Agents who are FSBO specialists know that if they stay in contact with For Sale by Owner homeowners, they will get listings.

While FSBO leads are better than cold calls, the most productive warm lead is the expired listing, in my experience.

Chapter 11
Target expired listings.

Listening to Floyd Wickman one day, I heard him talk about expired listings – those homes which had been on the market but did not sell. They're not anti-Realtor, Floyd explained, they hired an agent before, they most likely will again.

What's more, he continued, their motivation may have changed. They may have more urgency to sell now than they did when they first listed. Maybe they are selling to relocate for a new job in another state, or to get married ... or divorced. They may have a baby on the way and need a bigger house. They just lost six months on the market with their previous agent and they may now be under pressure to get it done fast. Maybe they already own another home and are making two house payments.

Expired listings are, in my view, the warmest leads and, even today, represent the best opportunity to make money *fast*. They want to sell and they listed with a Realtor before. They are probably ready to act now, not six months or a year from now.

A brief history of expired listings.

In the 1980's and 90's, competition for expired listings was intense. It was fertile ground for listings and the best-trained agents pursued them vigorously.

An agent who specialized in expired listings could count on easily getting 3 to 5 listings per week if he or she knew the right questions to ask.

Then, things changed.

By the late 1990's, answering machines, voice mail, caller I.D, the Do Not Call list and cell phones insulated sellers from Realtors calling to re-list their homes.

Working expireds became excessively labor-intensive. Scrubbing the daily list of expireds to ensure properties had not already been re-listed and deleting those on the Do Not Call list was a tedious process. Researching contact information for homeowners who no longer use hard-line telephones was nearly impossible. After hours of filtering and culling expireds list every day, there was barely time left to make prospecting calls.

Agents who had once made a living working expireds left to pursue less labor-intensive business. Some saw opportunities in the short-sale and foreclosure markets. Others redoubled their efforts farming or contacting past clients. Still others turned to the internet and social media to build their business.

Working expireds was destined to be a brief chapter in real estate history when ...

Things changed back ... almost.

Just when it looked like homeowners whose listings had expired were sufficiently insulated from Realtors' calls, some ingenious folks created software which does the research for you ... affordably.

Each day, these web sites identify expired listings and eliminate properties which have already been re-listed. They scrub the list of expireds against the Do Not Call list and search for working phone numbers for the owners, including cell phones.

Working expireds has been reborn as a viable lead source. Most of the agents who worked expireds ten years ago either a) restructured their business to pursue other opportunities, b) left the business by finding other careers or retiring.

Today, there is relatively little competition and what competition exists is from agents who have little or no training working expireds. With the right training, you can become the big dog in expired listings in your marketplace.

Web sites which are researching expired listings include:

- TheRedX – Real estate's #1 Lead Generation, Lead Management and Lead Research Company.

- ArchAgent – Property Marketing Resources for Real Estate Professionals.

If you are up to the challenge, working expireds is a great way to build your real estate career. You can improve your chances for success if you know how to work expireds.

Part III
Improve Your Game

■■■■■■■■■■■■■■■■■■■■■■■■■■■■■■■■

Chapter 12
Sharpen your axe.

Two lumberjacks, Lars and Sven, faced off in the annual wood-chopping championship. Lars was young and strong. Undefeated in 10 years, Sven, was a stark contrast. His hair had grayed and his hung over his gangly frame.

"He is old and weak," Lars muttered, " I am young and strong. I can chop for hours." Sure enough, Lars chopped and chopped and chopped. Sven was chopped, too, but every hour he would sit on a tree stump with his axe across his lap, sweating.

"Ah-hah!!" Lars exclaimed, "The old man is tired." Excitedly, Lars chopped even faster. When time elapsed, Lars gleefully threw his arms up in victory until, in disbelief, he heard, "And the winner is, Sven, our undefeated champion!"

Stunned, Lars looked over at Sven's pile of lumber. Sure enough, Sven had chopped more.

"How can that be?" Lars asked Sven, "When I looked over, you were sitting on the stump, resting. I kept chopping and chopping."

"I was sharpening my axe."

Before pursuing expired listings, make sure your axe is sharp.

Sharpen your basic telephone selling skills.

- Smile. People hear your smile over the phone. Keep a mirror at your desk so you can see if you are smiling or not. I'm serious. Look at it often. Are you smiling?

- Never cross your arms, even on the phone; it is a defensive posture and your defensiveness will come through.

- Speak clearly. Enunciate. Don't talk too fast. Listen to how the prospect responds to your voice. Speed up or slow down accordingly.

- Ask the prospect's permission to call him or her by anything other than their proper name. "Mr. Smith, may I call you Harold?" The prospect will usually oblige by giving you the name most people call him. "Well, folks around here call me Harry." Ask permission again. "So, may I call you Harry?"

- Don't presume that addressing the prospect informally is acceptable. Never presume someone goes by a common nickname. Calling David "Dave" without knowing it is a nickname he likes is simply rude.

82

- Wear a headset so your hands are free to take notes and look up information on the MLS while you are on a call with a prospect. Take a lot of notes.

- Always "ask for the order." The single biggest mistake agents make – even seasoned veterans – is not asking for the order. Be prepared to close for an appointment to meet face-to-face … if you want the listing.

Sharpen your knowledge of expireds.

If you choose expireds as your niche, learn everything you can about homeowners whose listings have expired – how they think, what they need and how to listen to them.

The highest level of competence is when you know what to do without thinking about it. Your responses become second nature.

Read every book and attend every seminar on working expireds you can find. Get the best sales training from world-renowned trainers – Floyd Wickman, David Knox, Mike Ferry, Tom Hopkins. Buy their DVDs and listen to them at home, in your office, your car, at the gym or on the walking trail. Steep yourself in the process. Become an unconscious competent.

Become an Unconscious Competent.

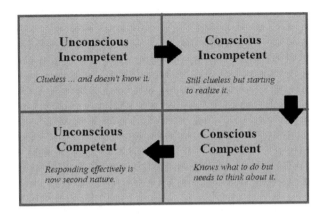

1. **The Unconscious Incompetent.**
   When they start in real estate, most agents are incompetent but they don't know it. There is bliss in ignorance ... just not much money. Unconscious Incompetents stumble aimlessly hoping to bump into a paycheck.

2. **The Conscious Incompetent.** After a few hard knocks, most agents start to understand how little they know. They become "Conscious Incompetents." You have taken a step up the evolutionary sales ladder but you are still a considerable distance from skill.

3. **The Conscious Competent.** With a lot of practice and experience, good agents reach a level of competence

... provided they think about what they are doing every step of the way.

4. **The Unconscious Competent.** How do you get to Carnegie Hall? "Practice, man, practice." A concert pianist doesn't think about which piano keys to play next; he practices until his subconscious mind takes control. Practice until your responses are a reflex.

Sharpen your pencil.

Maintain a log of your calls and their results.

- How many phone calls does it take to get a listing appointment?

- How many listings appointments does it take to obtain a good, saleable listing?

- What percentage of the listings you take will actually sell?

- How many listings do you want to sell in a year?

The most experienced, proficient agents have an exceptionally high hit ratio. Their goal is to sell 75% of their listings. They expect to come away from 50% of their listing appointments with a salable listing and they know it takes 30 - 50 calls to get an appointment.

Therefore, if you are really good at prospecting and you want to sell 45 listings in a year, here's the math:

- Selling 45 listings requires an inventory of 60 salable listings.

- Landing 60 listings means going on 120 listing appointments.

- Getting 120 listing appointments requires making 5,000 phone calls – roughly 100 per week. Every week. 50 weeks a year.

Starting out, your ratios won't be that high. You will list more homes which do not sell and you will lose out in listing appointments to other, more experienced agents. Simply put, schedule enough time to make more than 5,000 calls per year.

This is the reason setting aside blocks of prospecting time every week is so critical. On average, you can make about 10 phone calls per hour. In order to make 100 calls in a week – or more – you need to devote a minimum of 10 hours of your work week to active prospecting.

Break it down. Schedule two hours per day, five days a week, for prospecting. Twenty calls per day. Simple. The challenge comes when you get so busy that listing appointments and closings cannibalize your prospecting time. Don't allow it.

Prospecting is the lifeblood of your future business.

Sharpen your listening.

To work expireds successfully, you must be an exceptionally good listener and you must know when to keep your mouth shut – which is most of the time. For most of us agents, that's the hard part – keeping our mouths shut.

As salespeople, we are hard-wired to sell. It is what we do – we *sell* stuff. We persuade. We convince. We smile and shake people's hands. We tell customers about the features of our products and translate those features into benefits. We talk … and talk … and talk. We get in our own way.

> Never sell with "blah blah"
> when you can sell with "blah."
>
> ~ Floyd Wickman

Recently, a Realtor friend asked me to teach his prospecting team how to work expireds. His team is very successful working FSBOs, referrals and cultivating their farm. I met with each member of his team then took my friend aside and explained that only two of his four prospectors should ever work expireds. "Why is that?' he asked, surprised.

"Because only two of them want to learn to listen. The other two are eager to pounce with their salesmanship. They simply cannot stop themselves from jumping in and trying to fix a problem even though they don't know what the problem is. It is their nature. Keep them doing what they do well and let me teach the two who are capable of listening."

Some agents can learn to listen. Most can't. If you can, your opportunities working expireds are endless.

Practice listening to your children, your spouse and your co-workers. Stop yourself from trying to suggest solutions. Just listen. In addition to increasing your success with expireds, it will make your family and friends like you more.

Sharpen your customer service.

> Consumers are statistics.
> Customers are people.
>
> ~Stanley Marcus

Renew your commitment and understanding of exceptional customer service. Here are a few excellent books on raising the bar for consumer-centric marketing.

The Fred Factor
by Mark Sanborn

Raving Fans
by Ken Blanchard and Sheldon Bowles

Strive for excellence, not perfection. You are going to make mistakes. Forgive yourself. Learn from every one. Do your best to not make the same mistake three times. Twice is normal.

Sharpen your Technology Skills

Imagine taking your Toyota to the repair shop only to learn that the mechanic didn't own a set of those "newfangled" metric wrenches, just the good ol' American kind.

You probably wouldn't stay long let alone allow this outdated mechanic to work on your car.

Consumers expect their real estate agent to be current with the latest technology … and they deserve nothing less.

Are you still chained to your home computer … or worse yet, don't know how to use a computer at all?

Do you own a smart phone? A laptop? A tablet?

Do you know how to use real estate-related mobile apps like Google Maps, Google Earth, DocuSign, DotLoop, NetSellers, Goomzee and Realtor.com? How about photo editing programs like Aviary and Microsoft Picture Manager?

Do you know how to install and follow up with mobile text messages? Do you use texting as a contact method?

Are you engaged in social media to keep in touch with your database and know what is happening in their lives?

Every day, I hear all manner of excuses why agents are not learning and using today's technology, from cell phones and texting to electronic transaction management systems.

Change is inevitable. To stay relevant in today's business world, you must keep up with technological change.

Chapter 13
Working expireds is not
an art form.

Some trainers refer to the "art of working expireds." Prospecting expireds is not an art, it is a *process*. It is a process which requires knowledge of fundamental principles as well as well-defined objectives.

First, however, some absolutes:

Everybody's got an uncle in the business.

You will find yourself in competition for listings with agents who have more experience or have a prior relationship with the seller. Everybody has a second cousin or a retired aunt with a real estate license. Plan on it.

Know who you are going up against. Know which agents are the big dogs and, more importantly, know their strengths and weaknesses. Make sure you offer more of what the client wants.

Case in point: Early in my career, I discovered I was going up against one of the top agents in the city for an expired listing. I had no chance against this guy; he sold hundreds of listings every year. I had two. As I talked with the Seller, he explained one of his disappointments with his previous agent was that he never heard from him. (If

I had a dollar for every time I've heard that one …)

At the end of our meeting, I looked at him and asked, "So, which of us will have more time to call you with an update every Monday – me with three people to call or the other guy?" I called him each Monday morning until his house was sold … three weeks later.

List homes to sell, not sit.

In any market, your listings must be saleable. Too often, desperate agents take un-saleable listings in the hope that a) they might get a price reduction later, b) the seller will become more motivated and get the home market-ready, or c) pigs will fly. Too many agents settle for "c."

Pigs don't fly. Eventually, the listing contract will expire with the house unsold.

The listing will again be the target of agents who specialize in expired listings. Most often, the next agent will price it right and require the seller to make it marketable. They will cash the commission check – not you.

Walking away from a listing is a better choice than to list an overpriced or otherwise un-saleable property.

Re-Train your Brain.

Sometimes, other real estate agents perceive those who specialize in expired listings as vultures. They see them perched on a tree branch waiting for the listing to die before swooping down to feast on the carrion.

When I first started working expireds, other agents occasionally behaved as if I was taking food from the mouths of the agents who had the homes listed before. Soon, I began to see myself that way, too.

One day, a colleague asked me what I do. "Why, I sell real estate, you know that," I laughed.

"No, I know that. What I mean is: What do you do? When you walk in the office in the morning what is it you do?" he repeated.

"Ah! What do I *do*?" I realized he was asking me how I get business. How do I get new clients?

I looked at him and smiled, "I'm a vulture. I'm the guy who sits in a tree and waits for road kill. When a listing expires, I swoop down and carry it away."

"You like being seen as a vulture?" he responded, "and this works for you?"

"Pretty well, actually," I replied.

"Hmmm," he pondered, "Let's pretend you are a doctor and a mother brings her small baby to you, deathly ill. The baby is dying and she has taken the child everywhere to find a cure. You take one look at the baby and say, 'Do this,' and miraculously, the baby gets well and thrives. To that mother, are you a vulture or a hero?'"

It was an epiphany; it immediately changed my thinking. Realtors who get homes sold when other agents can't aren't vultures. To families who want – or need – to sell their homes, they are heroes.

Never feel guilty for pursuing an expired listing.

The first agent had the best opportunity to sell the home ... and failed. Now it's your turn. Never feel guilty about taking a listing away from an agent who was unable to do what he or she was hired to do – sell the house.

Never, never, never solicit an active listing.

Soliciting active listings is professionally unethical and offensive to homeowners whose homes are currently listed.

Remember, the seller chose the current listing agent. Prospecting during the listing is not only unethical it suggests to the seller they made a wrong choice to begin with.

Never, never, never berate your competition.

Take the high road … always. Don't take a cheap shot at your competition … ever.

Just as with soliciting active listings, berating your competition is both professionally unethical but it also suggests your seller made a stupid decision. It is a good way to shoot yourself in the foot.

Sell your strengths. Show what *you* can do for them, not what the other agent didn't.

> Always do right. This will gratify some and astonish the rest.
>
> ~ Mark Twain

Honesty and integrity still work.

Too often, I have heard real estate agents take the easy – and deceptive – approach to get an appointment with an expired listing.

They imply they have the "perfect buyer" for the home when they simply don't.

They get the appointment but lose the prospect when the conversation shifts from showing the home to the agent's imaginary buyer to signing a 6-month listing contract. The ploy is transparent and insulting to the seller's intelligence. Maintain your integrity; it will pay off in the long run.

Chapter 14
Now is your time.

> Luck is when preparation
> meets opportunity.
>
> ~ Seneca, Roman philosopher

Prepare your mind.

Before you sit down to the phone to make
your first call to an expired listing, get
yourself in the right frame of mind. In the
future, before every phone-calling session,
remind yourself of these truths:

- You provide an invaluable service and
  have a unique set of skills.

- You may be able to solve their problem
  when nobody else can.

- You are strong enough and confident
  enough to weather their rants, to listen
  carefully and stay focused.

Face the phone.

The time has come. If your palms sweat at the mere thought of picking up the phone to make prospecting calls, hot dog!! You're normal. Getting here sets you apart from most agents.

Keep it real. Be yourself. Stick to an outline but never use canned presentation. *Talk* with them. Listen. Have a conversation, don't play 20 Questions.

Pick up phone. Dial phone.

When the prospect answers, smile. Check the mirror. Are you?

Introduce yourself.

Tell them your first and last name and company name clearly. Always tell them immediately you are a real estate agent. Don't make the mistake of acting like you are a buyer who is interested in buying their home. (See "Shooting yourself in the foot.")

Keep your eyes on the prize. Focus. Listen.

Understand them.

First and foremost, you must understand the mindset of the homeowner whose home has not sold. Their emotions range from resignation to devastation, from disappointment to outrage. More often than not, they are angry. They are mad at the world, they are mad at their previous agent, they are mad at the market in general and they are mad at you. You may be the 10th real estate agent to call them this morning to re-list their home and their first questions typically are: "Where were you when we had their home on the market? Why didn't you sell it then?"

For now, forget about getting a listing. Forget about "selling." Your primary objective is to get them to talk. Picture the homeowner on the other end of the line as an over-inflated bag of air. Trust me. After a few calls to expired listings, the imagery won't be difficult to conjure up.

Understand they are angry. Often with good reason.

Let the air out.

Your first goal is to deflate the balloon. Listen to their rants. If you are able to get them talking – to offer your ear so they can vent their frustration – you are doing great. Keep going. As hard as it is sometimes, do not defend yourself, the other agent or the real estate business in general. Do not shut down. Stay open. Embrace their emotions. Recognize that although they are venting their frustration in your direction, *you* are not the source of their frustration.

Listen carefully and take notes. Lots of notes. Collect as much information as you can. You will need it later. Not yet. Soon. Ah! Ah! Shush. No selling. Not yet. Just listen.

Ask "open-up" questions.

Some trainers call them open-ended questions; Floyd calls them "wopens" because most of them start with the "w" sound – Where? When? Why? Who?

To me, they are questions intended to get the seller to open up to you – to answer more than "yes" or "no" and provide you with usable information. Whatever you choose to call them, they are powerful in understanding the seller's motivation.

Probing with open-up questions requires a bit of skill and a keen ear. If the seller believes you are using a script or a list of questions, they will assume you are just another boiler-room telemarketer. Rehearse every question until it flows naturally and genuinely.

Listen for cues. If you sense you are losing the seller while you are asking questions, vary the pace or change your tone of voice.

Ask the four critical questions. Get answers.

These are magic questions; the ones which, if answered, will magically put money in your pocket. Your objective now is to **get answers** to these four questions. No excuses.

1. Do you still want to sell?

2. When the home was on the market before, do you know why it did not sell?

3. How did you arrive at your price?

4. Could you go ahead with your plans if you do not sell?

Why are answers to these questions so important?

Question 1 – *Do you still want to sell?*

If they sincerely no longer want to sell, don't invest any more time. Before you know that, however, you must listen very carefully and understand the **meaning** of their words more than the words themselves.

If, for example, they answer, "No, I didn't get the job in St. Louis and that was the only reason we were going to sell" your chances of getting a listing is slim. It is not an objection; it is a condition.

On the other hand, if they answer, "We're going to hold off till spring" they have just told you, "Yes, we still want to sell. But not right now." (Shush. Shush! Don't try to change their minds. Not yet, not yet.) Write it down in your notes.

Ask them when "spring" starts in their minds. Never make assumptions; always ask. They may be thinking the spring market starts in January … or June. It will make a big difference in your approach.

Question 2 – *When you had your home on the market before, do you have any idea why it did not sell?*

This question elicits information about their previous experience on the market.

- How many showings did they have?
- What advertising was done?
- Do they feel their agent could have done more?
- What, exactly, did they want from their agent they didn't get?
- How many open houses were held?
- How many people showed up and what was the feedback?
- Do they feel the home was priced correctly?

Ask about the home itself:

- What is the condition of the home?
- Is there something they feel they should have done to the home to get it ready to sell which they didn't do?
- What is the color of the carpeting?
- When was the last time you wallpapered?
- What color are your walls?

You will be amazed at how much information you can get over the phone if you have been successful in deflating their emotional balloon. Your questions will show you are genuinely interested in helping them get their home sold.

One of my favorite techniques for discovering information about their home is to ask them to do me a favor: I ask "Will you take me on a walking tour of your home over the phone, starting at the front door? Will you walk me through your home and describe its colors, the carpeting, the layout …"

During one such telephone tour, a homeowner described his finished basement as having daylight windows. Since I was holding the previous agent's Multiple Listing printout in front of me while we talked, I stopped dead in my tracks. "Whoa! Hold on a sec, can you back up there?" I interrupted, "Did you just say you have a daylight basement?"

"Why, yes, of course, why?" he asked. I knew right then why his home had not sold. It was one of those rare times I closed for an appointment on the spot.

"If I could show you clearly why your house did not sell and I could fix the problem for you, would you consider meeting me in person?"

He was skeptical but agreed. When I arrived at the house, I showed him the Multi-List printout. The home had been listed with a "full" basement not a daylight basement. I explained the considerable difference it makes in appraisable value and marketability.

I took the listing and sold it seven days later … at full price. Even though the home had been on the market for 6 months, I sold it in a week because I kept digging until I uncovered a serious mistake the previous agent had made and missed for the entire 6-month listing period.

Question 3 – *How did you arrive at your price?*

This question is another way of asking, "How much money do you think your home is worth?"

More often than not, expired listings are overpriced and the homeowner is usually the one who set the price. Homeowners rarely answer, "The real estate agent did a Comparative Market Analysis and that's how we priced the home but we think it was WAY too high."

Ask the question. If the homeowners acknowledge the home was priced too high, they may be primed for a significant price reduction. It doesn't happen often but it does happen. Ask the question.

Usually, though, you will learn what you already suspect: The homeowner told the previous agent what he wanted to net and the Realtor, desperate to get a listing regardless of its price, took the listing knowing it was overpriced. Very often, the homeowner now blames the previous Realtor. In their recollection of events, it was often the Realtor who set the price and then pressured them to reduce it price later.

Turning away an overpriced listing is better than spending your money and energy on it. You will only disappoint the sellers when their home doesn't sell again.

That being said, getting a price reduction later is impossible if the listing isn't yours. Weigh your decision whether to take a listing on a) the likelihood of selling the home at the listed price and b) your chances of getting the price where it needs to be in order to sell.

Question 4 – *Could you go ahead with your plans if you do not sell?*

The homeowner's answer to this question reveals their motivation. If they answer, "We don't really need to move. We just want to see what the market will bring …" you do not have a motivated prospect. If, however, they answer, "We MUST sell!! We are moving to Des Moines next month," you may want to stick around and gather more intel.

Keep asking till you get the answers.

If the seller is resistant to answering these four questions, you have not deflated the balloon enough. Switch gears. Change the subject. Here are a few techniques for keeping the dialogue going without badgering the seller for an answer to any one question.

1. **Table the Topic.**

   Move on to one of the other questions but *always come back* to it. Put the question aside for the moment and when you come back to it, present it in a different form.

2. **Re-phrase the Question.**

   Suppose the seller responds to your question, "How did you arrive at your price" with "The agent set the price" and to your follow-up "So what do you think your home is worth?" with "You're the expert, shouldn't you be telling us?" By re-phrasing the question, you might get to the heart of the matter – knowing what they believe their home is worth. Here are a few ideas for re-phrasing:

"Now, your assessed value with the city is $50,000. Do you think your assessment is too high or too low?" Not surprisingly, most sellers believe their tax assessment is too high but their market price is too low.

Or, ask them, "Has a home exactly like yours sold in your neighborhood recently?" If the answer is yes, ask which one and look up the address on the MLS and find the sales price. You should not be surprised to discover the house they mention is NOT anything like the prospect's house but now will know what they are comparing it to.

Would you guess your home has more square footage than the average home in your neighborhood or less? Does it have special amenities which most homes in your neighborhood don't offer?

3. **Let's Just Say.**

One highly-effective technique is posing a scenario: "Let's Just Say." Despite tabling and re-phrasing the question, the prospect continues to be evasive about their reason for selling.

Try this: "Let's just say you list your home with me today and I sell it tomorrow. What would you do next?" The seller might reply, "We would look for a new place to live."

"And would that new place to live be a house or an apartment? Where? Would it be larger or smaller than your existing home? Will it have more or fewer bedrooms? In a subdivision or in the country?" Knowing their plans will help you learn their motivation.

Posing "Let's Just Say" is powerful in getting at the price issue, too. "Let's just say I listed your home at the same price as the previous agent – $299,900 – and two months from now, I bring you an offer for $265,000. Would you accept it or would you counter?"

Chances are, they will reply that they would counter the offer but if they answer, "accept it," you have just identified they will negotiate at least 12% off the asking price in order to sell the home. Make a note of the answer but don't use the information yet. Save it until you are face-to-face with them.

If they answer, "Why, counter it, of course!!" You could ask, "And what price would you counteroffer?"

Often, they will tell you exactly what their bottom line is and it is frequently considerably less than their previous asking price.

If your knowledge of the market suggests it will sell at $265,000, you may suggest pricing it at $264,900 for a quick sale. But not until you have seen the house and figured out *all* the reasons the house did not sell previously.

4. **Shot in the Dark.**

If all else fails, take a shot in the dark. Seriously. What do you have to lose?

"Based on what I know about homes in your neighborhood, your home is worth somewhere between $150,000 and $200,000. Am I close?" Predictably, the prospect will figure his home is on the higher end of that range. "Well, I suppose but I would never sell it for that!"

"Sell it for what?"

"What you said – $200,000." Rest assured sellers will almost never hear the low end of their price range; only the high end.

You now know the seller believes his home is worth more than the top of the range of other homes in his area. It's good information to know before you spend half a tank of gas driving to a listing appointment.

Decide if you want an appointment.

Now that you know

1) **If** they want to sell,

2) **Where** they want to go,

3) **How much** they want to get and

4) **Why** their home didn't sell,

you can decide whether you want the listing or not. Be honest with yourself. Do not take a listing just for the sake of having inventory.

Take a listing only when there is a high probability you will be paid.

> The Story of "No! Next!"
>
> A man walks into a busy
> New York City delicatessen,
> takes a number and waits on line
> until his number is called.
>
> "I'd like a pound of sliced
> turkey breast," he asks.
>
> "No!" barks the butcher, "Next!" and
> turns to serve the next customer.
>
> "Wait! You don't have
> any sliced turkey breast?"
>
> "No! Next!"

If the butcher had been a typical Realtor, he would have said, "Well, I don't have any sliced turkey breast but I have this nice roast beef, it tastes about the same, a little different color ..."

Real estate agents are optimists. How many times have we gotten the call from a buyer with bad credit and no money who wants to buy a 3-year-old, four bedroom, 3-bath home for $40,000? Instead of being honest with ourselves and saying, "No! Next!" we start looking for land contracts and foreclosures.

Know when to say no. Our human nature motivates us to help others. We want to help them with their dreams. Sometimes we can't. Identify a prospect's ability to buy or sell sooner than later.

If you want it, close for the appointment.

"Open-up" questions are specific for discovering information but closing questions are most effective to get decisions. Summarizing reminds the prospect why he should meet with you – that is, how you can help him achieve his hopes and dreams.

If the information you have collected causes you to believe you have a high likelihood to get paid, close for the appointment. Ask a question which has only two options: Yes or no.

"So, Harry, based on what we've talked about today, it sounds like you and Sally would like to sell the house and retire to Florida, maybe get a condo there so you don't shovel snow any more – if we can get your home sold. Yes?"

The question requires a yes or no answer.
Get the prospect to say "yes" before moving
on.

"Sure, we'd like to move to Florida. We
saw a little condo in Clearwater Beach the
wife liked. Not on the ocean but it was
close enough that we could walk to it ..."

"Harry, if I could show you that I could help
you to take the first step to get that condo in
Clearwater Beach, would you meet with me
in person?"

Again, it is a yes or no question. If Harry
balks, you have not yet discovered his level
of motivation. You need to go back to open-
up questions to discover his reason for
hesitating. Then re-visit the close by
summarizing again and asking for the
appointment.

Never, never, never ... never ... ask when
they would like to meet. It is an open-up
question and it gives the prospect the power
to deflect the conversation away from
making an appointment. Instead, give them
two options:

"So, would 7:00 p.m. work on Wednesday
or would Thursday at 6:00 be better?"

***Confirm that all decision-makers will be
there.***

Showing up to appointments without all decision-makers present usually results in wasting your time.

Make sure anyone who has a voice in the decision will be present at your listing appointment. If all parties who need to sign the listing contract are not present, you will need to schedule another meeting with them to review the entire listing presentation, pricing strategy, etc. If other family members have a say in the seller's decision, make sure they are there. This is especially true with elderly clients whose children are advising them.

Chapter 15
Prep the listing appointment.

Landing a listing appointment is Step 1 of the listing process. Step 2 is showing up.

Be prepared.

Most successful listing agents use a one-stop listing method. Go to the listing appointment with everything you will need to take the listing if you want it.

Previous listing history

- If the home was one the market previously, pull the history of the listing.
- How long has the home been on the market?
- With how many agents?
- What was the first listing price?
- How many times has the price been reduced?
- Are there identifiable mistakes in the listing information?

County records on the property

- What is the taxable value?
- Annual taxes?
- Any exemptions for primary residence?
- Deferred assessments?

- Delinquent taxes?
- Most recent sales price?
- What is the home's square footage, lot size, legal description and parcel number?

If you have a title company with whom you do business regularly, you may ask them to pull a listing package for you which will provide additional information: Outstanding mortgages – first, second, equity lines of credit – tax liens, homeowners' names of record, whether it is held in trust, whether a previous spouse may still have legal interest in the property.

Comparative Market Analysis

Know the range of prices in the neighborhood. Promise yourself to leave the Comparative Market Analysis in your briefcase unless you absolutely, positively MUST bring it out.

Getting bogged down in a microscopic comparison of all the homes in the neighborhood is a diversion from your objective: Getting the listing at a price it will sell.

The seller's motivation is more important than whether their home has a larger deck than their neighbor.

Listing Presentation

Bring your professional presentation of your qualifications, your company and your marketing plan is essential. Whether your presentation is in binder form or in video format on your laptop, make sure you have it.

Forms

Take all the forms necessary to take the listing if you want it. Fill them out beforehand with all the listing information – listing duration, legal descriptions, commission rate – everything except the price. You don't want an otherwise seamless listing appointment to suddenly turn bumpy because you are scribbling out forms.

Price is the only item you cannot fill in: you need to see the home first to know its market value.

As you will see later in this chapter, negotiating commission at the listing appointment is to be avoided. Presume you are worth whatever commission you charge. Fill it in on the listing form.

Keep blank pages of all forms in your briefcase just in case you need them.

Carry three pens

Yes, three. One for her, one for him, one for you. Yours is to use as a pointer as you present the contracts for their signatures. Theirs are to sign the contracts without them needing to hand one pen back and forth.

Writing tablet

Most people comprehend and retain information better when they see it. Learn to read upside-down. Learn to write-upside-down. If you can show your point in addition to saying it, you will give your prospect a better chance of understanding it.

Calculator

Take a calculator that is easy to use and easy to read. Trying to pull up the calculator app on your cell phone is cumbersome at best. So, too, is fumbling with a calculator which has tiny keys and screen. Simple ones with big keys and readout screen are great to use when you are meeting with sellers.

Complex calculators which can figure land contract amortization tables are great. Keep them in your briefcase or desk.

Be on time.

This should be obvious. Be on time. If traffic could cause you to be late, leave 20 minutes early. If you arrive early, park a couple blocks away. Pull up to the house a few minutes before your appointment.

If arriving late is unavoidable, call before your scheduled time and let them know when you will arrive. Never simply show up late.

Notice the neighborhood.

See what buyers will see as they drive into the neighborhood and toward the home.

- What is the condition of other homes nearby?
- Is the property in close proximity to industrial sites or main thoroughfares?
- Does the home have a nice view?
- Is the home downwind of a livestock farm or waste management site?
- Excessive noise is a huge turn-off to buyers.
- Do you hear barking dogs, loud music, or revving motorcycles and hot rods?

The seller may have no control over the neighborhood but the buyer has a choice whether to buy there. All other things equal, buyers tend to choose less noisy.

Notice the home's first impression.

- Does the home have a good first impression?
- Is the lawn green and lush?

- Is it mowed and the landscaping trimmed?
- Are the sidewalks and driveway cracked?
- Are the roof shingles beginning to curl or covered with moss?
- Is the home's exterior clean and fresh-looking?
- Are its colors outdated?
- Ring the doorbell. Does it work?

Control the appointment. Nicely.

When they invite you in, smile, shake hands and look them in the eye. Introduce yourself and guide them to kitchen table. Expect them to ask if you want to see the house. Say no. Explain you would like to get a bit of information first; to catch up on their experience when they had the house listed before. Give all decision-makers a business card. If their children are nearby, give them a card too. They will smile … especially if there is a shiny logo on it. It will also keep them busy while you talk with Mom & Dad.

Get acquainted. Have a conversation. Give them 5 minutes to relax. Then get down to business.

Tell 'em what you're going to tell 'em.

Any good business meeting has an agenda and everyone gets a copy. No surprises. Tell your prospects what you are going to talk with them about. They will feel more comfortable with you if they know what's going to happen. My agenda is printed and I share it at the beginning of the meeting.

1) Ask a few questions
2) Look around the house.
3) Show you what I will do to sell your home.
4) Provide ideas for improving marketability.
5) You decide & I decide.
6) Determine listing price.
7) Sign forms.
8) Review Showing Procedures.

1) Ask a few questions.

- What is your reason for moving?
- When do you want to move?
- What do you need in net dollars to make your move?
- How much do you owe on the home – first and second mortgage, equity lines of credit?
- Are you underwater on your mortgage and if so, how much?
- Have you considered a short sale negotiation of the underwater portion of your mortgage with your lien holder?
- What would it do to your plans if you could not sell?
- What do you need to know from me to make a decision to get the ball rolling tonight?

2) *Look around the house.*

Ask them to show you the house. **More specifically, ask them to show you the home as they would like you to show it to a prospective buyer.** They will point out highlights of the home you would have otherwise missed.

Ask them permission to critique the home. "If I see something that could make your home sell more quickly, would you like me to tell you?" In a quarter-century of asking that question, I have never gotten a "No." Pointing out fixable shortcomings is better received when they have given you permission to do so.

Take notes. Write down all the property information needed for the MLS data sheet – from age of the home to its type of exterior siding. Write down all your observations for improving the home's marketability.

Use a Property Marketability Checklist to ensure you don't miss anything which will help sell the home. (See Appendix A.)

One of the most effective techniques for getting a seller to make a necessary repair is Floyd Wickman's response, "I would." You notice a cracked window, for example. Without speaking a word, stop, look at it, peer at it from a different angle, then another. Start to walk away, then turn back and stare at the cracked window again. Eventually, the seller will ask, "Should I fix that?"

You nod and reply, "I would." These two words, strategically spoken, will put thousands of dollars in your pocket every year.

Thank you, Floyd.

Take photos now if the home is photo-ready.

If the home is ready to photograph, take photos now, preferably before you talk about your marketing plan. If the home is not ready to take photos, schedule a time now to do so in the future.

"If you decide on me as your real estate agent, when would it be a good time to come back and take pictures?"

If you use a virtual tour, schedule its production while you are at the listing appointment.

Find what's hinky.

Most expired listings are eccentric; they have unique – hinky – characteristics which reduce their market appeal. Keep your eyes peeled to recognize the property's eccentricities. These eccentricities – an unusual floor plan, small lot, expressway view, steep driveway, for examples – will have a negative impact on the home's marketability and consequently, the price.

Sometimes, you can identify these unique characteristics over the phone but most often, you will need to see the home personally to get a clear picture of the challenges you will face.

3) *Show what you will do to sell their home.*

Sell what you've got. If you are a newbie, your franchise affiliation and company's market presence may be your strongest asset. If you have 40 years of experience under your belt but don't know how to send an e-mail, focus on your experience. If you are a master at selling homes at open houses, show them how many homes you've sold on open house. If you have a bunch of designations on your card, communicate how your real estate knowledge will ensure a smooth transaction.

If you have the best marketing program for their home and can give them more exposure than any other real estate agent, prove it.

Have a real marketing plan.

In today's real estate environment, you are competing with agents who know how to market. It's that simple. If you are the agent who still can't send an e-mail, learn. Then make sure your marketing plan for your new listings includes:

- Internet marketing
- Open houses
- Social media marketing
- Electronic (e-mail) marketing
- Mobile Platform Marketing

If you have 40 years' experience, a bunch of designations, franchise support, working with a top company and a powerful marketing program, identify which is most important to the prospect. Sell that.

4) Provide suggestions for improved marketability.

Recommend home staging.

Home staging is important. Even homeowners who are certified interior designers have difficulty being objective about their own homes. Home staging's objective is to sell the lifestyle the home offers. Sell the sizzle.

In my experience, I have seen very few homeowners or real estate agents who did a very effective job of home staging. Hire an expert.

Give them a to-do list.

Give the seller a handwritten to-do list based on the notes you took or the Property Marketability checklist you filled out while touring the property. Steam-clean the carpeting. Replace the patio screen that the dog scratched. Pull out the overgrown, leggy shrubs and plant new ones. Re-paint the Pepto-Bismol® pink bedroom and swap out the harvest gold appliances.

Two years ago, I got a call from clients whose home I had sold 15 years earlier. They wanted me to help their children buy their first homes and I was thrilled to do so.

One day, Mr. Seller laughed and reminded me their home had been on the market for a year with the previous agent before they listed with me. He recounted that he was shocked when I handed him a two-page to-do list.

Two weeks later, he completed the list. One week after that, the house was sold.

Before presenting your marketing plan, get their agreement that they will do those things which will help sell their home. If they are unwilling to do them, your pricing recommendation must reflect the home's poor marketability.

5) *You decide & I decide.*

Weak agents go to appointments hoping the seller will decide to list with them. Strong agents know they have choice, too. If the property is not in marketable condition or is overpriced, strong agents know when to say no. Taking a new listing is a mutual decision – the seller's and *yours*.

If you want the listing, ask for it.

Close for the listing … now. No, you haven't discussed price. When it comes to picking their agent, price should be irrelevant. The following exchange is predictable. Become an unconscious competent with this dialogue:

You: "Based on what I've shown you, do you believe I am capable of getting your home sold?"

Seller: "Yes, you seem capable enough."

You: Great! Shall we get the ball rolling?" Reach for the forms you filled in before the appointment.

Seller: "Well, that depends on the price."

Stop. Act surprised. Really. As if you hadn't heard it a hundred times before.

You: "Oh, I'm sorry. Help me understand. Are you going to choose the agent who tells you the highest price or the one who will give your home the greatest exposure?"

Chances are, they will not answer the question. Instead, they will answer your question with a question:

Seller: "Where do you think we should price it?"

You: "I have a dilemma. There are a lot of agents who will tell you whatever you want to hear in order to get the listing. I want to tell you the truth but I worry that I could lose the listing to another agent who might tell you a higher price to secure the listing. Do you want me to lie to you or level with you?"

Seller: "Level with us."

You: "Fair enough. So, if I can show you the price range in which your home will sell and it's something you can live with, will you list with me?"

If their answer is anything but "yes," you need to consider whether the prospect is serious about selling or simply trolling for an agent who will tell them what they want to hear.

6) *Decide on the price.*

Let's be honest. A home is the single biggest investment most people ever make. Most homeowners know the prices of homes which have sold in their neighborhoods and they have a fairly good idea of the range of prices for homes like theirs. Your Comparative Market Analysis will have provided you the same information.

Avoid comparing the minute details of each home; keep your pricing discussion about the range of pricing, not a specific price for their home. The price you establish for their home will move up or down within the range according to their motivation to sell.

Price to sell. Don't play the negotiation game.

Seller: "We want to price it higher to leave room for negotiation."

You: "So if your real price is $200,000, you want to price it at $225,000 to allow room for negotiation. Do I understand you correctly?'

Seller: "Yes, something like that."

You: "I understand why you would feel that way. There are a lot of sellers who leave room for negotiation. It's why their homes are still for sale after 6 months on the market. My question is, "Do you want to *show* your home or *sell* it?

Seller: "Why, sell it, of course. But if we price it at $200,000, buyers will offer less."

You: "Maybe they will. Maybe they won't. You can always say no. The price a buyer offers depends on how motivated they are to buy your home and how many other buyers are competing for your home. You have a better chance of getting a full-price offer if you have two or three buyers fighting over it than if you're priced $25,000 high. Wouldn't you rather turn down 10 lowball offers than to never get an offer because your home is priced too high?"

Weigh your decision to take the listing on its condition, market appeal and the seller's motivation. Don't walk away from an otherwise saleable listing if there is a high probability of a price reduction later.

Include the appliances.

Always include kitchen appliances in the asking price. They add value and remove an obstacle to a Buyer buying your home.

Explain that they can always say "no" to the appliances if the buyer doesn't offer full price.

Include a home warranty.

For approximately $500, the sellers can protect themselves from a major furnace repair during the life of the listing and offer peace of mind to the buyer. Home warranties are worth the price in value-added marketability.

7) *Sign forms.*

Confirm the listing price: "So, shall we list it at $200,000?" Present the completed forms. Hand them pens. Direct their signature.

Some agents believe their job is done when they have the signed contract in hand. It is not. Your job is just getting started.

8) *Review Showing Procedures.*

- Explain to your new client how showings will be scheduled. Permit direct scheduling with Realtors, especially in busy markets. Agents who want to show your listing should be able to schedule showings directly with the seller. It will create more showings and more competition for their home.

- For the seller's convenience, I recommend putting a key box on every listing. Explain to them how it works.

- Review a printed list of tasks to keep the home ready to show. Leave a copy with them. Feel free to cut, paste and print the following one.

Be Ready to Show Your Home!

Keep your home ready to show with a few hours' notice:

- Maintain spotless bathrooms – sinks, countertops, mirrors, toilets, tubs and showers.

- Keep the windows clean, inside and out.

- Mow the lawn and keep shrubs and landscape trimmed. In winter, make sure sidewalks and driveways are shoveled and clear of debris.

- If you are a smoker, smoke outside for the duration of the listing.

For showings:

- Remove all pets from the premises for the showing. It is not the buyer's responsibility to make sure Fifi doesn't sneak out the door. Even the sweetest dogs can become territorial and have a hissy-fit while the buyers are trying to tour the home. Pythons and boa constrictors in glass aquariums are just plain scary.

- Vacuum and dust thoroughly.

- Make sure the kitchen is spotless and dirty dishes are hidden in the dishwasher.

- Open all the curtains. Turn on all the lights. Dark corners repel customers. Buyers don't care about your mood lighting or the neon beer signs in your man cave. They want to see if the walls have cracks.

- Make sure the home smells good. Eliminate pungent cooking smells. Empty the litter box, diaper pail and garbage cans. Air out the house, if possible. Use air freshener sparingly. Avoid plug-in air fresheners and strongly-scented potpourri or candles.

- Leave. Get out. Go away. Let the buyers buy. The worst thing a seller can do is hang around. Buyers feel uncomfortable enough going through someone else's home but to have the homeowner hovering about will make them leave quickly. Give them the chance to try your home on for size. Let them get comfy there. Encourage them to run the faucets, peak in the cupboards, and open and close the doors.

Exit graciously and quickly.

Now, your listing appointment is over.
Don't linger about. Thank them for
choosing you, put the key box on, plant the
yard sign and get out. Explain it is time to
get to work marketing their home.

Chapter 16
Get your listings sold. Fast.

Front-end load your marketing.

You will sell homes faster and at better prices when you blast out of the starting gate on full-tilt boogie. Within 24 hours of signing the listing:

- Upload the home's specifications (data sheet) and photos to the MLS.

- Schedule an open house for the earliest possible date.

- Promote your new listing on Facebook, Pinterest, Craigslist, LinkedIn and Twitter.

- Announce your first open house within 3 days.

- Send e-mail bursts to top agents on your MLS.

  According to the National Association of Realtors, 95% of real estate transactions are done by the top 5% of Realtors. If you maintain a database of the top 20% of Realtors in your area; you can be sure that your new listing will immediately reach 98% of your target market instantly.

- Send e-mail bursts to your database.

  Let your friends, family, business associates and web site visitors know about your new listing via e-mail. You never know when one of them might know someone who is looking for just that home.

  E-mail bursts have the added benefit of being a great prospecting tool. One day, I received a call from a homeowner who wanted me to list her home for sale. As is my custom, I asked her how she got my name. She explained I had sent her sister – who had visited my web site and lived 50 miles away – an e-mail about a new listing. Her sister forwarded it to another sister who lived in California, who sent it to the sister who wanted to sell her home. That one e-mail ricocheted across the country before it landed in my own backyard.

  The seller said, "THAT'S the kind of marketing I want!"

  That's the kind of marketing she got.

- Announce your new listing in your farm or ranch.

If you cultivate a farm or ranch, mail a "Just Listed" postcard to your farm or ranch within 5 days. Follow it up within a few days with an "Open House" announcement. When it sells, send a "Just Sold" postcard with a picture of the home and your contact information.

- Make buyers salivate. Sell the dream.

  Write mouth-watering advertising copy describing the lifestyle the home offers.

  Your MLS comment section, newspaper classifieds and Facebook posts should spend less time talking about the sticks and bricks – the number of bedrooms, baths and garage stalls – than how it delivers the lifestyle buyers want.

- Provide feedback quickly.

  After every showing and after every your homeowner is anxious to know what the buyer thought about their home.

  On my way home after every open house, I call the seller from my car to tell them how many people showed up and if any visitors showed particular interest.

When other agents show my listings, I request their e-mail address or fax number so I may schedule delivery of an electronic feedback form. There are several internet-based programs. Showing Suite is one of the popular feedback sites.

If you have not received feedback by the next morning, call the agent. If you wait any longer, they will have forgotten the property completely. Personal contact with the showing Realtor is vital to getting a clear picture of the buyer's and the agent's perspectives about the marketability of the home.

Give the completed feedback directly to the seller without editing. It is important the seller knows the hard truth about what buyers and other Realtors are saying about their home. You will do your sellers no favor to pull punches.

If the feedback indicates the price is too high, ask for a price reduction – every time.

Chapter 17
Lead the pack.

Consistently applying the ideas presented in this book consistently will get you headed in the right direction in today's real estate environment but it is just the beginning.

> The view only changes
> for the lead dog.
>
> ~ Norman O. Brown

Change is inevitable and is barreling at us at light speed – literally. The agent who will capture greater market share in the future is the one who breaks new ground in his or her approach to customer service and personal promotion.

Beware of complacency. Envision new opportunities.

Subscribe to Hubspot and Jeff Bullas' Blog to stay out in front of the latest innovations in blogging and social media marketing. Read authors like Brian Solis ("The End of Business as Usual" and "Engage") and Jay Conrad Levinson ("The Best of Guerrilla Marketing--Guerrilla Marketing Remix") to see how consumer behavior is changing and learn ways to adapt your marketing strategies to it. Another excellent resource is "E-Marketing (6th Edition)" by Judy Strauss and Raymond Frost.

Keep learning from the best.

- Ninja Selling Skills

- The Floyd Wickman Team

- David Knox

- Tom Hopkins

- Mike Ferry

None of the ideas presented in this book will work all of the time. All of them will work some of the time.

Work smart. Then work hard.

- Choose your path.

- Build synergy in your marketing communications.

- Prospect relentlessly.

- Provide your clients the best advice and superb customer service.

- Value your product and your time.

- Be the pack leader.

- Keep showing up. No matter what.

###

Appendix A
Property Marketability Checklist

Print this checklist as-is or customize it to make it your own. Carry it with you on a clipboard to and during the listing appointment. Check those items which need the seller's attention.

Neighborhood and Surroundings

What are your observations as you approach the home?

_____ Is getting into and out of the neighborhood easy or are there traffic snarls?

_____ Are the homes in the neighborhood in good condition?

_____ Are there homes in close proximity to the property which could negatively impact your listing's marketability – barking dogs, semi tractors, travel trailers or commercial vehicles parked in their driveways?

_____ Does the home's deck overlook an industrial park?

_____ Does the home conform to its surroundings?

_____ Is the home noticeably larger or smaller than the other homes in the neighborhood?

_____ Is its architectural style unusual for the area?

These factors may not be in the seller's control but deciding to leave the neighborhood is in the buyer's control.

<u>Front Exterior</u>

Colors

_____ Are the home's exterior colors outdated or faded?

_____ Do the colors have broad appeal?

The home's exterior must be crisp and clean. If they are not, repaint.

Roof

_____ Is the roof smooth and flat?

_____ Are the shingles starting to curl?

_____ Is moss growing on it?

_____ If the home has eave troughs, are they bent or crooked?

Landscaping

_____ Are the lawn, shrubs, mulch beds and flower beds neatly trimmed?

_____ Are trees overgrown or blocking the view of the home?

_____ Can they be trimmed or should they be removed?

Driveway and Sidewalks

_____ Are the driveway and sidewalk cracked or uneven?

Front door

_____ Is the front door a focal point?
_____ Does it catch your eye … in a good way?

If not, repaint or replace it.

Garage door

_____ Are there warped panels or peeling paint on the garage door?

In short, don't lose the buyer at the street. Make them eager to get inside!!

Interior

Clutter

Remember that clutter not only hides the positive features of the home but it is also distracting. Your objective is to keep the buyer's eyes focused on the home, not the seller's ceramic statue collection.

_____ Does the home look cluttered?
_____ Are the kitchen counters loaded with small appliances?
_____ Is the refrigerator covered with magnets and post-it notes?
_____ Does excess furniture or furnishings make the home seem cramped?

_____ Are the shelves throughout the home filled with knick knacks or family photos?

_____ Are the closets jammed with clothes?

_____ Are the basement and garage so full of stored items they appear small?

Odors

_____ Does the home smell bad?

_____ Does it reek of cigarette smoke?

_____ Pet odors?

_____ Cooking odors?

_____ Diaper pails or garbage cans?

Cigarette smoke and pet odors are the most frequent offenders but pungent cooking odors, diaper pails and trash cans and garbage disposers may be giving off odors to which the seller is desensitized. Tell them to wash or re-paint walls; wash all curtains, drapes and bedding. Use Febreze® on cloth furniture saturated with odor. The seller may need to replace carpeting if shampooing does not eliminate the odors.

_____ Do the basement or bathrooms have mildew odor?

Suggest using bleach or pine cleaner to clean them. Recommend they use a dehumidifier to keep those areas dry. (Remember, cleaning does not cure the cause of the underlying dampness or more serious, hidden mold. It only makes the home smell better.)

Cleaning

_____ Does the home look fresh and clean?
_____ Do the windows sparkle?
_____ Are the curtains and blinds crisp and dust-free?
_____ Are the wood floors polished?
_____ Is the carpeting shadowy in high-traffic areas and on stairways?
_____ Are there walls yellowed from smoke or dingy from age?

Wash the windows inside and out. Wash or paint smudges on walls. Clean curtains, drapes and mini-blinds. Buff up wood floors and shampoo carpets which appear shadowy from high traffic areas. Replace carpeting that is stained, worn, dirty or outdated. Recommend they paint walls which are shadowy or yellowed from smoke.

Décor

_____ Are the home's colors up-to-date?

If not, suggest they re-paint with current, neutral colors. Don't be afraid to add a little pizzazz by adding dense accent colors sparingly.

_____ Do the kids' rooms have bright colors or painted murals?

Buyers with young boys will see a paint job in their future if all the bedrooms are Barbie-doll® pink.

_____ Is there a lot of wallpaper?

Buyers hate removing wallpaper when they buy a home. Encourage your seller to remove excessive wallpaper. No wallpaper is best.

_____ Are the carpets in good condition and contemporary in style and color?

If the carpeting is avocado shag, it does not matter how well it has worn. Replace it, preferably with carpeting which appeals to most tastes. Avoid room-by-room carpeting. If most of the home needs new carpeting, it is best to re-carpet throughout with one neutral color. Add excitement with area rugs and throws. Steer clear of dark colors; they make rooms shrink.

Basement and Garage

_____ Are the basement and garage jam-packed with stored belongings?

Urge them to clear out everything they don't absolutely need. Throw away old paint cans; the colors won't match now anyway.

152

Wood scraps they have been saving to build a birdhouse should be tossed. Nobody wants their collection of nails, screws, bolts and assorted fasteners. Tell them to pack them away for their next workshop.

Mechanicals

While you are in the basement, check the mechanicals – furnace, electrical system, hot water heater, foundation and so on. You do not need a contracting license to see that something does not look right.

_____ Is there mold or mildew or evidence of water?
_____ Is there rust on the furnace?
_____ Is there caked-on lime where the humidifier drains or has leaked?
_____ Are there loose wires and open junction boxes?

If you have any reason to believe there is a problem, suggest the seller hire a licensed contractor to check it out further.

Buyers will not pay top dollar for money pits. Tell your sellers the truth: Fix the problems before you put the home on the market or be prepared to concede more than the cost of repair in the sales price of your home.

Back yard

_____ Is the back yard inviting?

_____ Is the deck worn and dull?
_____ Is the patio cracked?
_____ Are the fences in good condition?
_____ Does the lawn look lush and green?
_____ Are there overgrown trees and shrubs?
_____ Does the patio furniture enhance the back yard or detract from it?

Remodeling

When selling, it is best to redecorate, not remodel.

Occasionally, however, a home will need more than de-cluttering, cleaning and painting. In most cases, however, the seller will not recoup their investment in a kitchen or bathroom overhaul – new fixtures and appliances, countertops and tile.

_____ Is the kitchen layout non-functional by today's standards?
_____ Are the appliances well past their life expectancy?
_____ Do the kitchen cupboards and countertops need replacing?
_____ Do the bathroom tiles and fixtures show the age of the home?
_____ Is the floor plan of the home choppy or disconnected?

If the home's appeal is significantly hindered by an inconvenient floor plan or outdated kitchen and bathrooms, selective remodeling may be necessary to improve its marketability. If remodeling is required, be sure the investment conforms to the value of the home. Installing a Jacuzzi ® tub and Corian® countertops in a $100,000 home is not a prudent expenditure. Conversely, remodeling with cheap components in a $500,000 home will do more harm than good.

If you consistently take listings which are in marketable condition or priced to compensate for their limited marketability, your ratio of sales to listings will increase dramatically and quickly. So, too, will your bank account.

###

About the Author

Don Phelan is the Director of Career Development for Five Star Real Estate in Grand Rapids, MI, a company of more than 200 agents. Inducted into the RE/MAX Hall of Fame in 2004, Don has been a licensed real estate agent since 1987 and an associate broker since 1991. He has been named to RE/MAX International's Executive Club and 100% Club. He is a Graduate of the Realtors' Institute (GRI) and is a certified electronic marketing professional (e-Pro). In addition, Don has earned his accreditation as A Certified Residential Specialist (CRS) and an Accredited Buyer Representative (ABR).

Since 2003, he has helped clients design and launch web sites and has conducted seminars on internet marketing and social media marketing strategies. He is a staff writer and real estate expert on Knoji.com. Additionally, his real estate articles have been published in several real estate trade and business magazines.

Prior to entering the real estate business, he was a marketing strategist for two worldwide advertising agencies – J. Walter Thompson and Ogilvy & Mather – where he developed and implemented marketing strategies for clients which included Burger King, Ford Motor Company, Marathon Manufacturing Company, Dixie Federal Savings and others.

Acknowledgements

To Jeff – for his leadership and friendship.
To Dan – for his relentless coaching.
To Lorie – for her unwavering belief.
To Tammy – for being my thoroughly biased cheering section.
To Jen & Katie – for being my pride and joy.

Cover Design and Illustrations: Jim Anderson Design Group
Editor: Brett Beimers

Made in the USA
Charleston, SC
01 February 2016